Mary Wollstonecraft

Mother of Women's Rights

OXFORD
PORTRAITS

Mary Wollstonecraft

Mother of Women's Rights

Miriam Brody

OXFORD
UNIVERSITY PRESS

for Madeline and Anna—and their century of women

OXFORD
UNIVERSITY PRESS

Oxford   New York
Athens   Auckland   Bangkok   Bogotá   Buenos Aires   Calcutta
Cape Town   Chennai   Dar es Salaam   Delhi   Florence   Hong Kong   Istanbul
Karachi   Kuala Lumpur   Madrid   Melbourne   Mexico City   Mumbai
Nairobi   Paris   São Paulo   Singapore   Taipei   Tokyo   Toronto   Warsaw
and associated companies in
Berlin   Ibadan

Copyright © 2000 by Miriam Brody
Published by Oxford University Press, Inc.
198 Madison Avenue, New York, New York 10016
www.oup.com

Design: Greg Wozney
Layout: Valerie Sauers
Picture research: Lisa Kirchner

Library of Congress Cataloging-in-Publication Data

Mary Wollstonecraft
p. cm.
Summary: Describes the life of Mary Wollstonecraft, the first great English feminist, founder of a school in London, and author of the first great argument for the
education of women.
ISBN-13: 978-0-19-511968-8
ISBN 0-19-511968-1 (lib.)
1. Wollstonecraft, Mary, 1759-1797—Juvenile literature. 2. Feminists—Great
Britain—Biography—Juvenile literature. 3. Women authors, English—18th century—Biography—Juvenile literature. [1. Wollstonecraft, Mary, 1759-1797. 2.
Feminists. 3. Authors, English. 4. Women—Biography.]

HQ1595.W64 M37 2000
305.42'092—dc21
[B]   00-027269
9 8 7 6 5 4 3 2

Printed in the United States of America
on acid-free paper

On the cover: Painting of Mary Wollstonecraft by John Opie, around 1790.
Frontispiece: Another Opie portrait of Wollstonecraft from 1797 shows her
pregnant with Mary Shelley.

CONTENTS

Preface

"... she is alive and active, she argues
and experiments, we hear her voice and trace her
influence even now among the living."
                    —Virginia Woolf on Mary Wollstonecraft

One day in late August 1797, in the north London neighborhood of Somers Town, Mary Wollstonecraft felt the beginning of birth pains. She had already borne one daughter easily and had no reason to fear a second childbirth. She climbed the staircase of the home she shared with her philosopher–husband, William Godwin, and promised him cheerfully she would join him later at mealtime. Ten days later she died. Although Mary had expected the birth to be simple, in fact the delivery had not gone well. The medical help the late 18th century offered was primitive, and neither brought her relief nor spared her.

The young woman who died prematurely that September was the first great champion of women's rights in the modern Western world. On Mary Wollstonecraft's gravestone in St. Pancras's churchyard, next to her name, her husband had carved, "Author of 'A Vindication of the Rights of Woman.'" This was the essay that had made Wollstonecraft famous. While revolutions in the United States and France were demanding rights for men, she insisted on the rights of women as well. She wrote that women too had the right to be educated and to participate in the important work of reforming

society. When Wollstonecraft finished writing, her name was insep-
arable from the struggle for women's rights. Her readers either
hailed her as one of the brave generation of rebels who were ending
monarchies and building republics, or they scorned her as proposing
ideas so ridiculous and outrageous they could not be taken seriously.

One man who did take her seriously was the American patriot
Thomas Paine, who wrote the pamphlet *The Rights of Man*. Abigail
Adams, wife of the second President, John Adams, read and admired
Mary Wollstonecraft, as did Lucretia Mott and Elizabeth Cady
Stanton, both campaigners for the right of women to vote in 19th-
century America. In our own time Wollstonecraft's "Vindication"
has been called the first important argument for women's rights.
During the two hundred years since it first appeared in bookshops,
A Vindication of the Rights of Woman has never been out of print.
Across two centuries, whatever the political mood of the day, this
essay and the name Mary Wollstonecraft belonged in any debate
about human freedoms.

During the sad autumn days that followed Mary Wollstonecraft's
death, her husband comforted himself by writing a memoir of her.
When his work was published, his account of her life reminded
some readers that they disapproved of the way Mary Wollstonecraft
had lived as much as they disapproved of her writing. One such
reviewer wrote that the "events of her life . . . will be read with disgust by every female who has any pretentions to delicacy." Some
readers unfamiliar with the life of Mary Wollstonecraft must have
wondered what had been so shocking about her life that she
inspired so much anger.

The Smithfield market, in the neighborhood of St. Paul's Cathedral, sold cattle and sheep brought to London from the country. Improvements in agriculture during the 18th century so enriched the diet of this livestock that the weight of these animals doubled from the beginning of the century to the end.

"SWEET BEVERLEY" —MARY AND JANE

Mary Wollstonecraft's childhood was not happy. Her father was bad-tempered, unsteady, and drank too much. Her mother was weak-spirited and unsympathetic. Both parents doted on their eldest son, and Mary often felt ignored. To worsen this mix of storm and favoritism, the economic fortunes of the Wollstonecrafts, though they began well, declined continually through the years of Mary's childhood, mostly through her careless father's steady mismanagement.

Elizabeth and Edward Wollstonecraft were a young couple who had every reason to be hopeful about the future of their family when Mary, their second child and first daughter, was born on April 27, 1759. In these early years of their marriage, Edward and Elizabeth lived in London under the watchful eye of Edward's father. The source of the family money, Mary's grandfather was a weaver in Spitalfields. He had built up a thriving business in that eastern edge of the City that lay in the shadow of St. Paul's Cathedral near the Elizabethan Charterhouse School. Spitalfields was a neighborhood of silk weavers, many of them Huguenot refugees, Protestants who had fled persecution in France at the end of the 17th century. Mary's grandfather had come south to

The silkweaving trade was established in Spitalsfield in East London during the 17th century and continued as a household industry until the end of the 19th century. Craftsmen and their families, shown here in 1895, hired by master weavers like Wollstonecraft's grandfather, labored and lived together in cramped and noisy rooms.

London from Lancashire and had found fortune in the silk business, becoming in his time a master weaver. A master weaver bought the thread for the journeymen, who were members of the weaving guild, an organization of skilled craftspeople. The journeymen, in turn, brought the thread home, where whole families, men, women, and children, spun it into cloth. The journeymen would then return the finished goods to the master weaver. Mary's grandfather may have kept a loom or two on his own property, but he depended primarily on these domestic spinning industries, which were known as the "putting-out" system of manufacture. By organizing these piece workers on a larger scale rather than having each journeyman-craftsman deal directly with a client, men like Mary's grandfather could have amassed a considerable fortune by the middle of the 18th century, when Mary was born. This system flourished during Mary's childhood and young adult years, although during her lifetime, the practice of household manufacture was giving way slowly to the new system of factory labor with spinning machines run by waterpower and later by steam.

Mary Wollstonecraft's father, Edward, entered the silk-weaving business as a clerk working for his father. Contracted to assist him for a certain number of years, he kept the books and learned the trade. His father, who was a good business-man, clearly intended that his son continue in the family trade, but Edward aspired to more than putting out thread and balancing the account books. As he and his young wife, Elizabeth Dickson, arranged for the baptism of their daughter Mary at St. Botolph's Church in Bishopsgate, the main street of the Spitalfields neighborhood, Edward was planning to climb the social ladder by becoming a gentleman farmer, leaving the noise and grime of London far behind him.

Edward Wollstonecraft's London had not changed much since the Great Fire had swept through the crowded timbered houses around St. Paul's almost a hundred years earlier, leaving the neighborhood near Spitalfields charred and devastated. When the young Wollstonecraft family lived with Mary's grandfather, they would have made their home in floors above the shop offices on the street level. The first sounds and smells that reached Mary in the high windows of the weaver's home were of a great city. Down the narrow streets outside these merchants' houses, London refuse ran in malodorous gutters. Hawkers called out the prices of fruits and vegetables. Flower girls, pie men, and milkmaids crowded the passageways, alongside urchins, street singers, and walkers. Farmers drove cattle or geese to market; and coaches, wagons, and carts clat-tered against cobblestones and pavement. Here, still, was the London of the great agricultural fairs that celebrated the planting and harvest seasons with noisy, bawdy processions of jugglers and acrobats, giants and dwarfs. Londoners frankly preferred the out-of-doors. They happily conducted the busi-ness and pleasure of life in the street.

At the time of Mary's birth at mid-century, London was also the center of such great literary and scientific works that

Sir Isaac Newton, represented here by the engraver and poet William Blake, symbolized the Enlightenment belief in the orderliness of the natural world. The 18th-century poet Alexander Pope wrote, "Nature and nature's law lay hid in night / God said 'let Newton be,' and all was light." Wollstonecraft believed that "nature's laws" made women worthy of the same education as men.

the period has been called the Age of Enlightenment. The satires of the English poet Alexander Pope and the essayist Jonathan Swift had instructed readers while delighting them. Earlier inventions made new learning possible. With telescope and microscope, scientists could chart the stars and examine the earth. Small wonder that contemporaries were convinced that the light of reason and progress was overcoming the darkness of superstition and tradition. A few years before Mary's birth, the great lexicographer Samuel Johnson had published the first dictionary, bringing system and order to the English language. The Royal Society, dedicated to the advancement of learning truths about the natural world, had already been meeting for almost a hundred years. Even public executions of criminals, although still a form of popular entertainment, were declining, although young adolescent children might yet be hanged for petty thefts or forgery.

But with the seasons marked by the great carnivals, as they had been since medieval times, and families still weaving thread into cloth at hand-powered looms under their own roofs, ordinary Londoners were living as they had always lived. The London mob was drinking beer again, having given up the newly taxed gin that had them reeling drunkenly in the wretched alleys immortalized in the engravings of William Hogarth. All the while the mood for political change was growing. Clamorous and volatile, the urban mobs were demanding political power under the leadership of John Wilkes, a radical parliamentary leader. During Mary Wollstonecraft's infancy in Spitalfields, the London journeymen rioted when master weavers responded to a decline in the silk trade at the end of the Seven Years' War by reducing wages. In the 1780s, anti-Catholic mobs destroyed property and left 285 people dead. At century's end a hungry crowd demanding bread booed even King George III.

William Hogarth's engraving Beer Street *reflects the improved safety and health of mid-18th-century Londoners when they gave up the highly taxed gin for beer. During Wollstonecraft's lifetime, a better diet, more employment, higher wages, and advances in medical care also contributed to a better quality of life.*

Rather than this sometimes foul and belligerent city, Mary's father preferred what the poet William Blake called England's "green & pleasant Land," the gentle hills of the countryside covered in yellow gorse and thistles or in lavender washes of heather. By choosing the countryside, Edward Wollstonecraft meant to recast himself as a member of the gentry, the polite landed class of England. Members of the gentry made their money by renting their land to farmers or selling the crops they grew, rather than from manufacture and shop keeping. Edward's wife, Elizabeth, came from a family that had done well in the more genteel wine business in Ballyshannon, on the west coast of Ireland, and she was not likely to discourage his distaste for city life and city money: the greater the distance between themselves and the weavers' looms, the better. Unlike his merchant father, whose wealth came from trading cloth, Edward planned to invest the capital he inherited in land and hire farmers to work it for him. He would spend his time in gentlemanly pursuits such as the politics of village life and the sports of the leisured class—hunting, shooting, and drinking.

Unhappily for the Wollstonecrafts, Edward had not inherited either his father's habit of hard work or his business sense. To be sure, the times were not favorable for small farmers. Larger landholders could afford to invest in new mechanized equipment, and practice more scientific methods of draining and fertilizing the land and sowing the seed. Smaller farmers were not only unable to mechanize, they had less and less access to the common lands the villages had traditionally set aside for grazing farm animals. During the years Edward Wollstonecraft farmed, this common pastureland was increasingly enclosed and converted to richer, larger private property-holdings, leaving smaller farmers without grazing land. Under such conditions, smaller farms soon went under. The owners and their families were driven into the life of poverty of seasonally hired agricultural workers, ultimately becoming the laboring classes of the new factories.

Yet, Edward Wollstonecraft had the capital to be a successful farmer, if he had been willing to accept the advice of a knowledgeable manager, or if his temperament had been steadier and less self-indulgent. Certainly many other farmers had profited from land in the same regions where Edward Wollstonecraft had bought and then sold his property at a loss. At his father's death in 1765, Edward inherited his share of 10,000 pounds including the rental income from London property, grand sums he would gradually lose over the years of Mary's childhood.

Just a few years after his father's death, with a great deal of money still in his pocket, and after a few false starts on farms outside of London, Edward Wollstonecraft brought his young family to settle near the small country town of Beverley in Yorkshire. Mary was nine years old. Newly arrived in the north country, the Wollstonecraft family included the beloved oldest son, Edward, called Ned; Mary; two younger brothers, Henry and James; and two younger sisters, Eliza and Everina. Although the Wollstonecrafts left London happily behind them, they soon found that the York-shire winds blew more harshly than those in the temperate south, and that the rough fields were not so well-suited to farming. Moreover, a man of Edward Wollstonecraft's restless and social nature was drawn to the comforts that town provided. After a few years living on his own land, years that saw the birth of his last child, Charles, he moved his wife and seven children into Beverley. Beverley was a pretty Yorkshire town built in a hollow by the River Hull, where inexpensive, large, and even elegant homes were increasingly attractive to persons aspiring to gentility.

Beverley was the first home Mary remembered. She lived here another six years, until she was more than 15 years old. Never again would she spend so many years in one place. Though she learned to be a writer in London, she remembered fondly the Yorkshire countryside where she roamed the lanes and groves of Westwood, the park on the York road just beyond town. Rather than playing inside with dolls, Mary loved to join her brothers in the merry sports of outside play. Sometimes when she felt unnoticed and unloved at home, she roamed alone in the fringe of trees at Westwood—all that remained of a once-great forest that had reached to the edge of town. Writing later about her childhood, Mary reminisced that when she was by

In the 19th century, Victorian brick buildings stood near the timbered medieval houses and 18th-century stone dwellings of Wednesday Market in Beverley, Yorkshire. When the Wollstonecraft family lived on this square, farmers sold produce and livestock at market on Wednesdays, while the bells of the magnificent nearby cathedral told the hour.

herself, she made up songs to angels whom she pretended were visiting the earth.

Mary was an imaginative and sensitive child for whom the natural world was alive with feeling, these feelings reflecting her moods as if the woods and lanes were alive with a beating heart and a human soul. Later, she recommended playing out-of-doors to any ambitious girl, since she was convinced that outdoor exercise was responsible for the development of resourcefulness and intelligence in women. In all of her adult writing she praised fresh air and regretted the social practice that kept young girls inside, learning traditional women's skills and social graces, such as needlework, piano playing, and dancing. She was happiest when she was remembering Yorkshire, with its open fields, parks, and woodlands.

When the Wollstonecrafts moved from the farm into town, they took a house in an old square called Wednesday Market, where Georgian stone dwellings were slowly replacing medieval timbered houses. From Wednesday Market, Mary could hear the bells of the church of St. John the Evangelist tolling the quarter hour from its tall medieval tower. Beverley was a sociable town, especially for gentry families. An assembly had recently opened, a social gathering place for families who paid a subscription fee so they could dance, play cards, and drink tea, coffee, or hot chocolate. Beverley also boasted a theater, a racecourse, and a circulating library, which offered the latest books for a fee. These attractions lent Beverley a dignity and gentility that made the town appealing to families such as the Wollstonecrafts, who were happy to forget the clamor and odors of London. From her parents Mary learned a genteel snobbery that took the form of a lifelong hostility to making money from trade. From her girlhood in Beverley she acquired a lifelong belief in the simple, restorative quality of fresh air and the wisdom of letting young girls run loose outside.

Mary had her first and only formal education in Beverley. She attended a day school, where she learned simple skills of arithmetic, geography, some French, music, and dance. Ned meanwhile was sent to a more serious grammar school that had a library. Most children of the middle classes, certainly most girls, had little schooling. No one particularly expected girls to learn more than the basic education that Mary's school provided. If they were interested, and if their families owned books, girls were permitted the free run of the bookshelves in their own homes. In that way they might try to teach themselves what their brothers learned at school. By the time Mary Wollstonecraft wrote *A Vindication of the Rights of Woman,* she was widely and richly read, and so able to refer to a good range of literary and historical works. But she acquired this knowledge on her own and informally by associating with intelligent and well-read people.

In Beverley, Mary made her first important friend, Jane Arden. Jane's father gave lectures on astronomy to interested people in the community, including young people like

The Royal Society was founded in London in 1660 to study the natural world and understand the laws that governed all forms of life. Reading papers to each other about experiments they performed, Royal Society members advanced knowledge in this Age of Enlightenment, a time of confidence that increased learning would improve humankind.

Mary. The Ardens were a poor but distinguished Beverley family with an intellectual and religious background. Dr. John Arden was a member of the Royal Society. He popularized astronomy for his neighbors so that ordinary persons, even if not particularly fortunate in their birth, could improve themselves. Like other Enlightenment thinkers, John Arden believed society would progress as people became more learned.

Mary began to correspond with Jane in 1773, when the two girls were in their early teens. Jane had gone to nearby Hull to visit an aunt, and Mary had promised to write her. She was excited and apprehensive as she launched her first correspondence. Jane's family had a higher social standing in Beverley than the Wollstonecrafts, and Jane already had a few other girlfriends. Self-conscious about her own writing and worried about the impression she would make, Mary told Jane in her first letter, "I have just glanced over this letter and find it so ill written that I fear you cannot make out one line of this last page, but—you know, my dear, I have not the advantage of a Master as you have, and it is with great difficulty to get my brother to mend my pens."

Writing itself was no easy matter. The quill pens writers used during Mary's lifetime needed endless repair and sharpening. But a more painful self-consciousness than faulty pens can account for explains Mary's apology. She was moody and introspective. In her first two letters she painstakingly copied out the familiar ballad of "Sweet Beverley," about the town's beauties, and other local poems for Jane's amusement rather than trust herself to original composition. Mary was making a bid for Jane's respect and friendship, and hoping that the young girls Jane had already befriended would not mean more to her than Mary herself. At the same time, Edward and Elizabeth Wollstonecraft would have welcomed this friendship. Mary lived at a time when adults encouraged young girls to turn their affections toward one another. Parents felt that these sentimental girlhood friendships were far safer for young unmarried women than were romantic intimacies with boys. Staying home from church one Sunday morning, Mary began her first letter to Jane.

Dear Miss Arden

According to my promise I sit down to write to you

"My promise and my faith shall be so sure

"As neither age can change, nor art can cure

"Perform thy promise keep within faith's bounds

"Who breaks his word, his reputation wounds."

Inclosed you will find "Sweet Beverley" for meeting with an old copy, and being in a hurry I thought you would excuse the badness of the writing.—

"True ease in writing comes from art not chance

"As those move easiest who have learnt to dance."

MARY WOLLSTONECRAFT TO JANE ARDEN

Mary Wollstonecraft was 14 when she began a correspondence with her girlhood friend Jane Arden. The pattern of taking offense easily and withdrawing with hurt feelings marked all of her close friendships. Mary and Jane mended their quarrel quickly. Wollstonecraft wrote this letter from Beverley, sometime between June 4, 1773, and November 16, 1774.

Miss A.—Your behaviour at Miss J——'s hurt me extremely, and your not answering my letter shews that you set little value on my friendship.—If you had sent to ask me, I should have gone to the play, but none of you seemed to want my company.—I have two favors to beg, the one is that you will send me all my letters;—the other that you will never mention some things which I have told you. To avoid idle tell-tale, we may visit ceremoniously, and to keep up appearances, may whisper, when we have nothing to say:—The beaux whisper insignificantly, and nod without meaning.—I beg you will take the trouble to bring the letters yourself, or give them to my sister Betsy.—You never called yesterday; if you wish to be on the least friendly footing, you will call this morning.—If you think it worth while, send an answer by my sister.

M.W.

I assure you I expect a complimentary letter in return for
my staying from church to day—

I should likewise beg pardon for not beginning sooner
so agreeable a correspondence as that I promise myself
yours will prove, but from a lady of your singular good
nature I promise myself indulgence—

Mary's worry that her bids for affection might be rejected
continued throughout her life and plagued most of her
friendships and romances. At 14 years of age, moving from
girlhood into young womanhood, she may have worried
about how she looked, how intelligent she sounded, how
worthy of love she was. She had bright auburn hair, large
expressive eyes, and a broad brow. In later years she excited
the admiration of many men, including a whole generation
of younger poets, who admired her face and her brains. But
her parents believed Ned was more important and Eliza the
family beauty.

Hypersensitive to her own faults and painfully vulnerable to slights, real or imagined, Mary wished intensely to
improve herself. The Ardens, concerned about Jane's education, which they themselves were supervising, seemed
achingly different from her own parents. Kind Mr. Arden
was already lending Mary essays to read, while her own
father scoffed at the idea of a girl wanting education.
Although Mary's family had more money, the Ardens were
scholarly and well respected. The Wollstonecrafts were
quarrelsome, and already her father's bad temper and debts
were attracting notice in the town. Later in life Mary would
tell her publisher, Joseph Johnson, a man who was always
kind and protective of her, that she "never had a father."
Nor was it clear, from the way she remembered her own
childhood, whether she ever had a mother.

Edward Wollstonecraft was violent when he drank, alter-
nately given to what Mary remembered as "fits of kindness
and cruelty." When he drank, he directed his random blows

at his wife or the children. Mary, fearful for her mother's safety, crept down the hallways at night to take up a station outside her parents' bedroom door, ready to hurl herself between them if her father became brutal. Her father's anger could be triggered quickly and for trivial reasons. To her terror and horror, he was cruel to his animals, kicking them aside when they annoyed him, and once, in his anger, he may have hanged one of his dogs. Such moments froze themselves in his daughter's memory, and recalling them years later, Mary again felt "abhorrence" and "agony." Her response to her father's violence was a lifelong crusade against unreasonable authority.

On the other hand, this sometimes abusive, sometimes loving, hard-drinking cavalier of a father cut a dashing figure. His children found him bewildering, maddening, and hurtful. In fact, Mary more closely resembled her moody, unpredictable father than she did her mother. Elizabeth Wollstonecraft was an unappealing figure in her daughter's eye, someone who sank under Edward's abuse, moaned over his extravagance but failed to rally to help her children or alter the tone of her unhappy household. She seems to have been a passionless and plaintive woman. In her efforts to attend to her large and boisterous family on a declining income, she was demanding and intolerant of her growing daughter in ways Mary could not later forgive. Both parents openly favored their firstborn, Edward, the son whom Mary described later in her fictions as the "heir apparent" who took advantage of his preferred position. Certainly Elizabeth may have demanded more of her oldest daughter and tried to restrain the high-spirited nature of the child, which was Mary's most singular character trait in her adult years. Sadly, Mary felt she was not much indulged or loved as a child. She believed she was given unreasonable commands and was expected to obey seemingly unfair orders without question, such as having to sit quietly in her parents' presence for several hours without speaking a word.

Years later, when Mary Wollstonecraft sat down to write her first novel, she called the fiction *Mary*, and frankly poured forth the memories of her childhood. Her heroine was the daughter of an "Eliza" and "Edward," as she had been. Mary wrote that the fictional Edward was "very tyrannical and passionate; indeed so very easily irritated when inebriated, that Mary was constantly in dread lest he should frighten her mother to death." Although the fictional Mary struggled to be tender toward her mother, her kindness was not returned. Worse, this Mary herself sometimes had a violent temper. "She saw her father's faults, and would weep when obliged to compare his temper with her own." After such a storm, she prayed to heaven for forgiveness and vowed to watch herself carefully "to save herself this cruel remorse."

This intense, self-examining, and judgmental daughter was not easy to raise. Undoubtedly when her mother was searching about for help with the younger children, Mary was away, either singing to angels in Westwood or racing through the lanes with Ned and Henry, tearing her petticoat and losing the ribbons. Then again, that violent temper may have asserted itself when Mary's mother told her to sit quietly. Compared to the genteel and reasonable Ardens, how flawed and unseemly her parents appeared to her, what an agony of shame and fear her father's drunkenness. Describing herself in this autobiographical fiction, Mary says that when her fictional counterpart felt contempt, "few could stand the flash of her eyes." Mary was probably a handful, and her mother may have felt appalled by the flashes of anger and derision she sometimes saw in her oldest daughter's eye. Yet as Mary wrote later in her autobiographical novel, "Could she have loved her father or mother, had they returned her affection, she would not so soon, perhaps, have sought a new world."

At home Mary learned that she could never depend on love. In the world she turned to she was relentless in searching for love she could trust, but never trusted that she had found it. After Jane returned from Hull the two girls passed letters back and forth between their houses, often using their young sisters as couriers. Mary gossiped with Jane and quoted poetry to her, occasionally preaching as well about the importance of friendship. She exaggerated any slight and responded instantly with scolding and hurt feelings.

One day Jane declined Mary's request to sit next to her at church, apparently because Mary had recently exchanged heated words with an Arden sister. Jane must have been afraid the two girls would resume their quarrel in church. Mary was outraged that her friend "insinuated that I dared to have prophaned so sacred a place with idle chit chat." She declared their friendship over and accused Jane both of preferring other friends and also ungenerously exaggerating Mary's faults. It was a silly quarrel, a storm that passed quickly and soon Mary was writing to "dear Jenny" again. But in the heat of the quarrel Mary had written, "I keep your letters as a Memorial that you once loved me, but it will be of no consequence to keep mine as you have no regard for the writer." In fact, Mary did not save Jane's letters, but Jane held on to Mary's all her life.

When Mary penned her first letter to young Jane Arden, she broke off her postscript, saying, "Please write back. I have a hundred things to add but can't get time for my Mama is calling me." Searching for a companion to hear these "hundred things," Mary made her first tentative step beyond her family. The search for an audience to hear her out and to love her back became work that she carried far beyond the "sweet Beverley" of her childhood and to much larger audiences than Jane alone.

2

FANNY—AND
A ROOM OF
THEIR OWN

In the spring of 1775, when the roads had been cleared of
snow and fallen limbs, Edward Wollstonecraft packed his
family into a stagecoach and their belongings into a wagon,
and removed them from Beverley. Mary would have seen
the tall spires of Beverley's medieval cathedral from the hollow in the hills as the coach made its way south past
Westwood's green park.

If Mary knew, she never explained why her father left
Beverley, although townspeople had been gossiping, Edward's
business affairs were in disarray, and everyone knew about
his drunken revels. Once again, Edward claimed that a profitable opportunity lay ahead of him. He relocated the Wollstonecrafts to Hoxton, a not particularly attractive suburb of
London, hoping to reclaim the family fortune.

When the Wollstonecrafts moved to Queen's Row in
Hoxton, they found the Clare family living next door to
them. Mr. Clare was a clergyman. He was an odd-looking
man—short, sickly, and deformed, with a large head on frail
shoulders. Perhaps because he was not well, or perhaps simply because he was unusual, Mr. Clare almost always stayed
inside his house. He so infrequently sallied forth that he was

able to wear the same pair of shoes for 14 years without them showing signs of wear. Like Mr. Arden, the Reverend Mr. Clare was a learned man. He and his wife took a kindly interest in the young girl who lived next door.

Before long, Mary was spending whole days, even whole weeks, at the home of the Clares. She loved their conversations about poetry, as well as their gracious manners. The Clares took up Mary's education where the Ardens had left off. Just as Mr. Arden had provided essays for Mary to read, the Clares recommended "proper" books to her and asked her to read them aloud to them. As she did, Mary would hear her own voice strike the sound and rhythm of the English language as if it were music written by the finest composer—fine training for any writer. To be sure, she needed a friend to write to and to write about. The Clares also provided a friend for Mary, although they could not have known how important and precious this gift to her became.

One day, when Mr. Clare had decided to take a walk, he brought Mary to meet a family he knew who lived in the south end of London. The two of them stopped at a small house, and Mr. Clare took Mary inside a carefully and neatly furnished room. Here Mary was struck by a sweet domestic scene that she never forgot: a slender, elegant young girl was busily "feeding and managing" younger brothers and sisters. As Mary wrote later in her fiction, this girl's "refinement" and "taste" caught her eye, and she "eagerly sought her friendship."

The young girl was Frances Blood, who at 18 was just a little older than Mary. She was called Fanny, and was the oldest daughter of parents of Irish descent who were falling short of money. The history of the Blood family's misfortune echoed familiarly for Mary. Mr. Blood had married a woman with a dowry, a sum of money a father gave to his daughter when she married. But Mr. Blood spent most of his wife's money and had left Ireland deeply in debt. Mary thought Mrs. Blood was pleasant, although a little dull, and certainly too passive when she might have been forceful. Still, the Bloods were a more peaceful family than Mary's. Mary liked Mrs. Blood and even called her "Mother." She drew close to all of Fanny's family, charmed by the self-sacrifice of Fanny, who sold her drawings, and of her mother, who did needle-work in dim light that was ruinous to her eyes. Fanny seems to have been a talented young woman, who sang and played well and drew "with exquisite fidelity and neatness."

Mary loved Fanny all her life and cherished the memory of her friend after Fanny's death. She named her first daughter for her and wore a ring made of Fanny's hair that her second daughter, Mary Godwin Shelley, inherited. For many years this friendship was "the ruling passion of her mind," because Fanny represented to Mary an ideal of intelligent feminine devotion, directed to the well-being of people she loved. Fanny was another and more important Jane. When Mary described "Ann" in her fiction *Mary* as the friend with whom she shared a girlhood correspondence, she fused memories of Jane and Fanny; but after writing *Mary* it was only Fanny whom she meant when she wrote about friendship. Fanny became the model on whom she based many of the fictional characters who were meant to represent virtue, such as Mrs. Trueman, a character in a book Mary later wrote for children:

> Her voice is sweet, her manners not only easy but ele-
> gant . . . her little ones hang on her hands. . . . Drawings
> . . . ornament her neat parlour; some musical instru-
> ments stand in one corner; for she plays with taste, and
> sings sweetly.

Because Mary and Fanny did not live very near each other, they could not visit as frequently as they would have liked. Instead, they wrote to each other, and once again Mary cast herself in the role of student. Fanny wrote so much better than she, Mary felt her friend must teach her accuracy and style. But again Mary worried that she was only second-best. Perhaps, she fretted, Fanny did not always return her friendship as intensely as she herself offered it.

Fanny had already fallen in love. Although she was without dowry and her health was weakened by the labor of keeping her family afloat, Fanny hoped to marry Hugh Skeys, a young Irishman with a good income. The few years between Mary and Fanny occasionally yawned like a chasm, for, as Mary remembered herself later, at sixteen she was still a "wild" though animated girl, fresh from the Yorkshire countryside. Unsophisticated and intensely romantic, Mary idealized friendship. Having a young friend like Mary Wollstonecraft would have been work.

Mary would never take love or friendship halfway. She must imagine her love as perfect; and if her fantasy of perfection broke under the strain of everyday life, she faced the reduced dimensions of her friend with disappointment and injured reproof. Mary wrote that "Ann," that fictional combination of Jane and Fanny, often hurt her. "When her friend was all the world to her, she found she was not as necessary to her happiness. . . . Very frequently has she run to her with delight, and not perceiving any thing of the same kind in Ann's countenance, she has shrunk back; and, falling from one extreme into the other, instead of a warm greeting that was just slipping from her tongue, her expressions seemed to be dictated by the most chilling insensibility."

Gentle Fanny must have wondered at the mood swings of her friend. Fanny's lungs were weak. Waiting eight long years for Hugh Skeys to marry her while the Blood family teetered on the brink of misery, Fanny was often melancholy as well as sickly. In her elegance and delicacy, Fanny was irresistible to Mary, who responded again and again to Fanny with tenderness, even though she was irritated and wounded by Fanny's patient attendance upon Hugh Skeys. Yet, after modeling her correspondence on her friend's superior style, Mary gradually realized that she was intellectually superior to Fanny, and perhaps emotionally stronger as well.

There was a resilience in Mary, a determination not to be wholly trod upon, a spirit that she may have inherited from her more competent grandfather. She probably did not see this spunkiness in Fanny. Although she was still a "wild" and unmannered Yorkshire girl, Mary gradually found in herself a will to grapple with all of the troubles that came her way. Whatever the future might hold for her, Mary wanted Fanny in it. Writing to Jane Arden four years after the Wollstonecrafts arrived in Hoxton, Mary told her old friend about her new one. She has found, she wrote, someone "whom I love better than all the world beside, a friend to whom I am bound by every tie of gratitude and inclination." Imagining her own future, which she must try to bend to her own desire, she told Jane, "To live with this friend is the height of my ambition." Here Mary paused: perhaps the unmixed happiness of living with Fanny would not be worthy of the moral person Mary wanted to be. She added, "And indeed it is the most natural wish I could make, as her conversation is not more agreeable than entertaining." Mary reread her sentence and reconsidered. Was entertainment an appropriate goal for as serious a person as she was? She crossed out "entertainment" and wrote in "improving." Pleasure was all very well, but a virtuous person should always wish to improve herself.

With America on the brink of revolution on the other side of the Atlantic as Mary passed into her 16th year, she may have walked by William Godwin on the street, because he too was living in Hoxton. Young Godwin was a student at a dissenting academy. These intellectually prestigious schools were established by the thriving Protestant merchant classes called dissenters because they disagreed either with the doctrines or practices of the established Church of England. Barred by Parliament from attending the older established universities of Cambridge and Oxford, English dissenters established their own centers of learning. Later in his life, Godwin wondered what might have happened if he, a bookish young man of 20, had met Mary, the high-spirited girl from the country, while they were both in Hoxton.

The interior of an 18th-century dissenters' meeting house. Philosopher William Godwin was educated to be a dissenting minister like his father and grandfather before him, but instead became a religious sceptic, placing all his hopes for social progress in human reason.

As Godwin was fond of giving sermons at that time in his life, and Wollstonecraft not so interested in hearing them from solemn, self-absorbed young men, in all likelihood they would have passed each other by. Mary did not stay in Hoxton long, and she never met William Godwin there.

Meanwhile, Edward Wollstonecraft's economic speculations, whatever they may have been, had come to naught. Only a year after arriving, he decided to try farming again. This time he moved his family to Laugharne, a small sea town in Wales at the mouth of the Taff River in Carmarthenshire. Wales was far from Fanny's home in London, and Mary yearned to be nearer her and more distant from her own family. Still, this coast of Wales was wild and romantic country with its own ruined castle that had housed knights in Elizabethan times and had been stormed by Cromwell's men in the 17th century. Roaming the caves in the sea cliffs, Mary heard new melodies in the Welsh language and admired the proud traditions of even the simplest people who lived in huts near the coastline. These were scenes and sounds to be stored for use in the fiction she would soon be writing.

But the farm imposed more cramped quarters on the Wollstonecrafts, and Mary was restless for privacy. She wanted a room of her own, where she could store her books and paper and pens. How could she write in a crowded room with her brothers and sisters all about her and her mother calling on her for help?

Nor was the removal to Wales any more satisfying to Edward Wollstonecraft than farming outside Beverley had been years earlier. Gambling and mismanagement had eroded his capital dangerously, and his money was running out. Some final miscalculation, perhaps even something criminal, suddenly hastened Edward's descent into calamity.

In financial disarray, the family moved back to London only a year after leaving. This time, the Wollstonecrafts settled in Walworth, near Fanny's home. Undoubtedly, Mary had prevailed in the choice of location. She had made an odd bargain with her parents: she gave up her slim expectations for financial independence in exchange for some authority within her parents' home. In his panic, Edward had demanded her inheritance from her. Mary willingly gave up her share of the money that probably had been left to the younger children by their maternal grandparents. Certainly their paternal grandfather was not the source of this legacy. He had passed over his son's daughters and younger sons in the longstanding tradition of English primogeniture, which required that only the first born son should inherit the family money. This system assured that family fortunes remained substantial, rather than becoming depleted by being divided among all of the children. Brother Ned, who inherited the legacy from his grandfather, was studying to become a lawyer and on his way to being married. He was only too aware of how precarious his inheritance was because of his father's mismanagement. Ned was increasingly unwilling to offer any money toward the upkeep of his parents' household or to assist in Edward Wollstonecraft's luckless schemes. In this crisis, Ned may have contributed something or even been bilked of some of his inheritance, for even years later he was still paying off debts. Mary gave up her money, but in return insisted that she be given her own room in Walworth.

Even with such a room, life at home was intolerable. Without a farm to manage, Edward Wollstonecraft faced the destruction of his hopes with angry drunkenness and blows directed at the long-suffering Elizabeth. Even Mary's closed bedroom door could not shut out the unhappiness of this marriage. Mary announced to her parents that she wanted to make her own way and leave home. Her parents responded to this declaration with dismay and indignation. Elizabeth clung to Mary and begged her to stay. With her beloved Ned on his own, Henry gone, and her two younger daughters at school in Chelsea, only the spirited Mary stood between her and Edward. Mary could not resist her mother's pleading. Although she had found a prospect for employment, she put it aside.

When Mary cast about her for a way to leave her family, she found that her situation was not favorable. If their father's plans to rise into the class of the landed wealthy had been at all successful, the Wollstonecraft daughters would have been given a generous dowry and married to a landed, even perhaps a titled, husband. Mary must have wondered what was to become of her. Angrily, she had vowed that she would never marry, and in all of her fiction there is no situation she prefers to describe more than the misery of someone whose marriage is arranged by her parents. While it would be nice to marry for love, who would have her without money? Wasn't Fanny Blood still waiting for Hugh Skeys?

Surely, she had to learn to earn her own keep. But there were not many occupations a young woman could enter and still be considered a lady. Although Mary hated pretense and ignorance, polite society was still important to her. Jane Arden was already a governess, but Mary did not have enough education to hire herself out as a teacher. The only genteel employment open to her was as a companion to an older woman. To be sure, to become either a companion or a governess was a sorry lot. A companion was dependent on the whims of an older woman who might be demanding and unsympathetic, the companion always at her beck and call with little time for herself. A governess had to tolerate the whims of rich people's spoiled children. In both situations, the young women were lonely, without family or friends of their own; despised as social inferiors by their employers; and with no end in sight to their dependency. Charlotte Brontë's *Jane Eyre* described the misery of the governess, while her fellow Victorian novelist George Eliot, in her novel *Daniel Deronda,* described Gwendolyn Harleth rushing into a disastrous marriage with a man she loathed in order to avoid becoming a governess.

In 1778, when she was 19 years old, Mary left home, in spite of her mother's pleading and her father's disapproval. She left to become the companion of Sarah Dawson, an elderly and quarrelsome woman who lived in Bath, a fashionable resort in the west of England. Mrs. Dawson had already retired several companions, whom she had undoubtedly exhausted, when Mary came to her. But Mary, who had just won a victory over her parents, resolved not to bend to any new tyranny. She meant to make her new situation tolerable by being firm with Mrs. Dawson, and she rather liked the idea of being successful in the job where other young women had not been. By all accounts, she managed well, because Mrs. Dawson later confessed that Mary was the only companion who had made her feel she had to be more careful about how she behaved.

Mary came to Mrs. Dawson in the spring. The older woman was living at her son's home in the center of Bath. A greatly varied and sociable parade of people came to this elegant resort, presumably to drink the healthful waters of its thermal springs. The Romans had built and loved this place when they came to Britain in the first or second century AD,

The Royal Crescent of Bath reflects the 18th-century ideal of beauty as an ordered and restrained repetition of architectural forms. When Mary Wollstonecraft came here as a young woman, she wrote to a friend that Bath "was a most delightful place" with "the most regular and elegant buildings" she had ever seen.

during the days of their empire. Now 18th-century visitors meant to have a good time while drinking the waters. From the East Indies and the United States came clerks, land managers, planters, and hucksters. From all over Britain came well-to-do tradespeople, members of the new professional classes, landed gentry with or without aristocratic titles, and even royalty. They came to gamble their money if they had it or recoup their fortunes if they had lost them, to dance in the assembly rooms, and to gossip with one another at tea the next day.

Fortune hunters hoped to meet young women with dowries, and debutantes hoped to make a suitable match. Elegant masters of ceremonies presided over the assembly rooms. They required that men not wear swords and that once the minuet began, all dancers rotate so that no one would have special privileges because of an aristocratic title. By day the social set could stroll along the splendid crescent rows of Georgian town houses, nodding gracefully to friends who passed by, and leave calling cards at some houses to signify they had dropped by and would welcome a return visit.

With all of this, Bath must have been dispiriting for young Mary Wollstonecraft. She was, after all, no debutante daughter herself, although she might have been. She was a poor, dowerless dependent who had to sit beside Mrs. Dawson in the assembly rooms, bring her tea, and comfortably arrange her chair. Mary must have been tapping her feet to the music under her long skirts, and her sharp eyes would have missed none of the flirtations going on about her. If her father had been a better provider, she would have been among that bevy of marriageable young women. She described herself as being "a still life" while the minuets were playing. She liked Bath well enough. As a city, it was certainly better than London. But she preferred the country, she was lonely, and she missed Fanny.

Only two months after Wollstonecraft arrived, she received some good news. She learned that her old friend Dr. Arden was in town, giving a series of lectures on philosophy and offering geography lessons. Mary rushed to his residence, hoping to find Jane, but her friend was in Norfolk,

At the fashionable resort of Bath, men and women gathered at the Old Pump Room to socialize while drinking the healthful natural waters. With better roads and vehicles available, crowds of patrons came to Bath, where such splendid interiors flattered their own sense of importance.

working as a governess. Mary wrote a long, chatty letter to her, giving her the grim news of her family and its misfortunes, teasing her about boyfriends, and confiding in her about her friendship with Fanny. But, behind her resignation to her new situation and the debacle of her family's hopes, Mary complained of headaches, fatigue, and phantom body pains. Mary wrote as if she were already an old woman. Now 20, she no longer expected a happy life, she said. Happiness was only a dream.

Jane must have found Mary's letter alarming. She wrote back, asking with some concern after Mary's health and wondering what had happened to her vivacious Yorkshire friend. Mary's next letter was more hopeful, although the change in her mood was not long-standing. She had spent a good summer at the seaside town of Southampton with the Dawsons. Mrs. Dawson had sent her ailing companion to the doctor, and he recommended bathing, which Mary found bracing and revitalizing. Mrs. Dawson was really not so bad. Mary told Jane that her employer was intelligent and had "seen a great deal of the world," so was someone from whom Mary felt she could learn. Once back in Bath, though, she was prey again to her old melancholy. The minuets were tiresome, and the promenades around town were too familiar. A learned woman had said of Bath that the only thing one could do that one had not done the day before was to die. Oddly it was a death—her mother's—that brought Mary home again to her family.

Elizabeth Wollstonecraft had fallen seriously ill, and she was a long time dying. This unhappy woman had known only disappointment in her marriage, mixed with fear of her bad-tempered husband. As their circumstances became more dire, she had spoken to her daughters wistfully of a cottage in the United States, where they might start all over again. But there was no new beginning for Elizabeth and Edward Wollstonecraft. Elizabeth was afflicted with dropsy, a disorder that swelled her body with fluids, while Edward, having

A Letter from Bath

While a companion to an elderly woman in Bath, Wollstonecraft met the Arden family again and resumed her correspondence with Jane. Writing in May or June of 1779, she tells Jane the news of her family since they had left Beverley, describing the melancholy that frequently overcomes her. As she wrote, she revised her letter, crossing out one word and replacing it with another.

It is almost needless to tell you that my father's violent temper and extravagant turn of mind, was the principal cause of my unhappiness and that of the rest of the family.—

The good folks of Beverley (like those of most Country towns) were very ready to find out their Neighbours' faults, and to animadvert on them;—Many people did not scruple to prognosticate the ruin of the whole family, and the way he went on, justified them for so doing:—a pretended scheme of oeconomy induced my father to take us all into Wales,—a most expensive and troublesome journey that answered no one good end.—Business or pleasure took him often to London, and at last obliged him once more to fix there.—I will not say much of his ungovernable temper, tho' that has been the source of much ~~uneasiness~~ misery to me;—his passions were seldom directed at me, yet I suffered more than any of them—my spirits were weak—in short, a lingering sickness was the consequence of it, and if my constitution had not been very strong, I must have fallen a sacrifice long before this.—as it is, my health is ruined, my spirits broken, and I have a constant pain in my side that is daily gaining ground on me:-My head aches with holding it down, I wrote a long letter before I began to write to you: I am tired so good night.

squandered his fortune, railed against his wife that her ailments were surely imaginary.

When Mary first returned, Elizabeth had been distant toward her. After all, Mary had left home, had gone to Mrs. Dawson in Bath, as if she had not still been needed so badly at home. Mary's mother had ignored her while she was with Mrs. Dawson, declining to write her letters or to be remembered to her when Everina wrote. Just as she had when Mary was a child, Elizabeth wanted her to feel her disapproval as a cold absence of affection.

However, when Mary returned home to nurse her mother, the two found a way to repair the breach that had separated them. This was no easy nursing. Elizabeth was peevish and wretched, probably subject to the anguishing thirst of her ailment. But in her great need, Mary's mother at last accepted the tenderness her daughter had always longed to show her. Alas, her illness was fatal, and Mary could provide little more relief than when as a child, she had readied herself to stand between her mother and her father's blows.

Elizabeth's decline was slow, taking a year and a half. Grown so used to Mary, she refused to accept food from anyone else. The exchanges between mother and daughter must have implied gratitude and love. Mary herself was exhausted from administering the purges that dropsy required, and Elizabeth came to know that this high-spirited, rebellious daughter possessed vast reserves of loyalty and resourcefulness. In her quiet moments, Elizabeth must have wondered why the 23-year-old Mary had so willingly given up her independence to remain at home.

As her death approached, Elizabeth counseled Mary, "A little patience and all will be over." Her mother's final words engraved themselves in Mary's memory, and in her fiction she offered them again and again. In the novel *Mary* she recreated her mother's dying moments and included the words she may have longed to hear as well.

"My child, I have not always treated you with kindness. God forgive me! Do you? . . ."

"I forgive you!" said she, in a tone of astonishment.

Perhaps they uttered such words, for some kind of healing peace at last passed between mother and daughter. Though Mary forgave the mother she loved, she never accepted that the humiliation Elizabeth had endured during her life with Edward was ethical. If this were marriage, she would have none of it.

After Elizabeth's death in 1782, the Wollstonecraft family broke apart. Edward was inconsolable with grief at her gravesite. However, he was not a man to tolerate the anguish of self-evaluation. Soon he married a woman who worked as a housekeeper, appalling the Wollstonecraft children by his speed and his choice. Physically ruined by alcohol, nearly destitute, and increasingly unable to manage his own affairs, Edward took his new wife and his youngest son, Charles, back to Laugharne in Wales. Ned, now acting as the head of the family, doled out an allowance to his father and invited teenaged Eliza and Everina into his home. James went to sea to become a sailor. No one ever mentioned Mary's brother Henry, about whose fate little is known. Mary moved in with Fanny Blood's family, where she sat up until dawn with Mrs. Blood, doing needlework to bring in money.

Another crisis loomed not very long after. Eliza Wollstonecraft, beauty of the family, had at 19 attracted the attention of Meredith Bishop, a young man from a prosperous shipbuilding family. Although she was without a good dowry, Eliza became engaged to him, pleasing the entire Wollstonecraft family. Mary believed she herself would never marry, but she understood the advantages of marriage for Eliza, who was clever but less ambitious than Mary. Moreover, Mary believed the tenets of her Anglican faith, that the married state was, for most women, the acme of worldly ambition. "My sister has done well," she wrote to Jane

Arden, "and married a worthy man whose situation in life is truly eligible." She confessed with amusement that her little sister would have a higher social status as a married woman than Mary herself.

Mary's attitude toward married life was mixed. Her parents had given her a poor model of marriage with their shrieking and cringing, their exchanges of blows and lamentations. Small wonder that Mary wrote about marriage with amused contempt. When she told Jane about Eliza's marriage, Mary reminded her friend that Jane's sister too had been recently married and was probably back from her honeymoon. About this marriage, Mary wrote:

> The joy, and all that, is certainly over by this time, and all the raptures have subsided, and the dear hurry of visiting and figuring away as a bride, and all the rest of the delights of matrimony are past and gone and have left no traces behind them, except disgust: I hope I am mistaken, but this is the fate of most married pairs. . . . for which reason I will not marry. . . . I, like a true born Englishwoman, will endeavour to do better.

Even Mary, who believed married happiness was short, could not know how few months of bliss were in store for Eliza. Ten months after her marriage in 1782, Eliza bore a daughter and suffered a devastating postpartum depression. At the time no one understood that such disorders are prompted in some women after childbirth by the sudden alterations in their body chemistry. Eliza's illness was sudden and terrifying, and there was no apparent cure. Mary, who came to help after the birth, wrote anxiously to Everina that Eliza's "ideas are all disjointed, and a number of wild whims float on her imagination." Eliza's first symptom was deafness, followed by "raving fits." Mary passed the maternal advice—"patience, patience,"—on to Everina, but she was growing seriously alarmed.

Alone with Mary, Eliza complained to her sister about her husband, saying she had been "ill used." At first Mary took these complaints to be a sign of her sister's malady. Meredith Bishop was a robust and self-confident man, fierce about having his way but also affectionate and kind. Mary, in fact, liked her brother-in-law. She appreciated his concern for Eliza as he kept himself away from her while she was so disturbed about him. Mary pitied Meredith when Eliza refused to see him. She thought he was unsteady and self-indulgent, like her father, but still a good man, even a generous one. He gave her 20 pounds for the Bloods when she told him that they needed some money. However, as her illness continued, Eliza confided to Mary that she wanted to escape her marriage. Perhaps no daughter of Edward and Elizabeth Wollstonecraft could move into married life without anxiety. Meredith Bishop now repelled Eliza. While Mary was reluctant to accept her sister's wishes, she at last became convinced that Eliza's very life depended on her leaving, in spite of her husband's refusal to let her go.

"Escape" was what they planned. There were no simple exits from a marriage in the 18th century. If a man had been "cruel" to his wife, badly beat her, she could separate from him legally. Meredith Bishop had not been cruel, and English law required that Elizabeth stay under her husband's roof and accept him into her bed, performing the duties of a married woman. If she left her husband, she would be fleeing illegally, because she belonged to her husband as if she were his property. Also she would have to give up her child, since the children of a marriage, along with the wife's dowry, belonged to the husband. By law, a married woman had no real existence in the community. In legal terms, she had disappeared into her husband when she married, and he represented all of her interests. Less than 10 years later, when Mary Wollstonecraft wrote *A Vindication of the Rights of Woman,* she stormed against these laws. They could have both sisters imprisoned: Eliza for leaving Meredith Bishop's household and Mary for planning her sister's escape.

Selling wives—as depicted in this 1832 broadside—was never lawful, but it was a popular means for a man to announce he was ready for a second marriage at a time when legal divorces were difficult and expensive to obtain. All her life Wollstone-craft argued against the marriage laws, claiming that women who were economically dependent on their husbands might as well have been sold into marriage.

"Those who would save Bess, must act, not talk," she wrote to Everina.

They fled in the morning in a carriage, both laden with all the clothing they could carry. Eliza gnawed on her wedding ring in distraction. Under assumed names, they took rented rooms in the town of Hackney. It would have been unwise to go to Ned, although he was sympathetic, because Meredith Bishop would have hunted them down there. As it was, Mary's heartbeat quickened with every carriage that rolled by her window, lest it be Eliza's husband come to take his wife back.

This was a daring escapade and so grave in the eyes of society that years later William Godwin did not mention it in his memoirs of his wife, lest he harm the reputation of the still-living Eliza. Mary's friends were solicitous. Mrs. Clare came to visit the two women in Hackney, bringing them a pie and a bottle of wine. Mr. Blood offered them his roof. But a cordon of sympathy formed around the injured husband, including, to Mary's ire, Fanny's longtime suitor, Hugh Skeys.

As she gave the news with sarcasm to her friend Jane, Mary knew she would be the "shameful incendiary in this shocking affair of woman's leaving her bed-fellow.". Since she meant to save Eliza, though, the risk was worth taking. Her sister improved and was well again. Moreover, Eliza seems never to have regretted the move she made. Even in her older age, she shared the female Wollstonecraft aversion to marriage. But what were these young women to do next? How were they to live?

Eliza told Mary she was willing to become a school-teacher, a prospect Mary was considering as well. Looking about her, Mary realized she was surrounded by young women who needed to be doing something. Fanny was still unmarried. Eliza and Everina were at loose ends. As for Mary herself, her mother's death and her father's remarriage and move to Wales had cut any lingering tie she had had with her past. Again Mary needed to act and not simply talk. Jane had written that she was planning to open a school in Bath with her sisters. Mary took Eliza at her word, and she too opened a school. She was 24 years old. It was time to begin her own life as she meant to live it.

THE APPRENTICESHIP AS GOVERNESS AND SCHOOLTEACHER

"With economy we can live on a guinea a week, and that sum we can with ease earn."

—Mary to Everina Wollstonecraft

Newington Green was a pleasant, tree-shaded suburb of London when Mary Wollstonecraft, her sisters, and Fanny Blood opened a school there for young girls in 1784. Newington Green was north of the city, and removed from its clamor and bustle. Hospitable villagers grazed their sheep on the green under the gaze of grand old houses with large, elegant windows. Into one of these houses Mary moved with her hopeful female household. Not one of them was concerned that they had few qualifications to teach school.

In fact, teaching school was a last resort for young women without money, and no one expected such teaching to provide any child with an education. Wollstonecraft herself believed a serious education was the responsibility of a child's parents. She disapproved of indifferent parents who sent their daughter to a day school rather than do the work themselves. She understood the commonplace belief that the schoolteachers of any young girl were little more than babysitters,

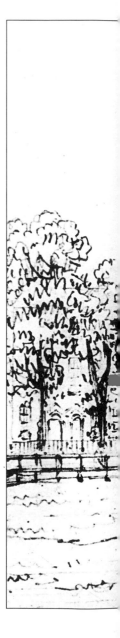

The modest Dissenting Chapel of Newington Green still stands today, flanked by the taller 18th-century residences that frame the square. Although she admired the minister, Rev. Price, Wollstonecraft disliked the simplicity of the chapel, believing a more ornate church was more likely to inspire spiritual feelings.

who were expected to manage the awkward years between a girl's infancy and her marriage with instruction in those decorative skills that polite society regarded as feminine. She would argue against this belief, but she was not yet ready to provide its alternative. Fanny could teach drawing, and all of them could teach at least reading and writing.

Fanny Blood had been worried about Wollstonecraft's grand plans. She felt an earlier idea, that they might earn enough by taking in needlework, was woefully naive. Fanny had suggested that instead they might open a shop and sell hats and perfume. But a school required less money to launch than a shop, and a friend of the Clares had come forward with a loan. When Mary moved Fanny and her sisters into one of Newington Green's generously proportioned houses, she easily collected 20 students for instruction, plus a woman with three small children to rent their extra rooms and help defray the expenses of servants and food. Mary Wollstonecraft was now a schoolmistress and a manager of a boarding house.

She may have known no Latin and little French or philosophy, but Wollstonecraft believed she was a good teacher: patient, reasonable, and affectionate. She claimed later that any student she taught remembered her and loved her. Eliza, emotionally fragile, was too unreliable to be a good teacher, and Everina was becoming infamous for her bad temper. Poor Fanny was tubercular and weak. Only Wollstonecraft's ambition and confidence held the school together. Barely able to pay her creditors, she nevertheless dispensed money generously to a host of dependents, including her father, who was still in Wales and always needy. She gave money also to the large and improvident Blood family, whose welfare she shouldered as if she had been born to them.

But Newington Green was far more to Mary than a place where she kept a school. Happily, she had settled in one of the most intellectually vigorous and convivial neighborhoods in all of Britain. Just across the Green was the

Dissenting Chapel, a simple and unpretentious church that had stood there since the early days of the 18th century and stands there still. Newington Green was a center of Unitarians, Quakers, Presbyterians, and Congregationalists, those dissenters whose great grandparents had colonized North America and whose cousins had helped to create the American Revolution. Indeed the Reverend Richard Price, who preached in the Newington Green chapel, corresponded with the American patriot Benjamin Franklin. A small man with a gaunt face, now in his 60s,

Richard Price was known for being the kindest of men. He was so benevolent that he freed small birds he found tangled in nets while he was out walking, and gently righted any hapless beetles struggling on their backs that he happened upon along the way. No surprise, then, that when he met Mary, he took an interest in the bright young schoolteacher so determined to make her own way in the world.

In addition to being a clergyman Price was a philosopher and an economist; and, in an age of agitation for political reform, he was one of the most vocal and eminent of spokesmen. By the time he met Wollstonecraft he had already recommended the abolition of the House of Lords, that group of titled men who held power in the government only because they were born to aristocratic fathers and not because they were particularly good or intelligent. An opponent of all inherited privileges, Price supported universal male suffrage at a time when only men with landed property could vote and vast numbers of educated men as well as all women, rich, poor, young, old, learned and ignorant, could

The Rev. Richard Price was so widely admired in America for his political observations that he was awarded a Doctorate of Laws by Yale University and even invited to come to the new nation to take charge of the American economy. When Wollstonecraft read Price's defense of the French Revolution, she was glad that "a glimpse of the glad dawn of liberty rekindled the fire of youth in his veins."

not. Richard Price believed that a moral and scientific education could make all people capable of wise self-government.
Such education would ultimately produce a harmonious and
ethical political community.

Listening to the Reverend Mr. Price from the pews of
the small chapel in Newington Green, Mary Wollstonecraft
absorbed lessons in political philosophy that would become
the cornerstones of her own argument for women's rights.
Her mother had suffered all through her marriage under the
arbitrary and despotic powers of her father. Wollstonecraft
herself had protested against the inherited privilege of her
oldest brother, Ned, who now possessed the legacy of their
grandfather while the Wollstonecraft sisters worried about
paying the next month's rent.

While Wollstonecraft found a friend in Newington
Green who helped her continue her education, her friend
Fanny was nearing the end of her life. Fanny's longtime
suitor, Hugh Skeys, was now a merchant in Lisbon, Portugal.
He had set a wedding date at last, and Fanny departed to be
married. Writing to Fanny's brother George Blood, Wollstonecraft expressed happiness for her friend, although she
was convinced that if Skeys had claimed Fanny sooner, her
health might have been stronger. Years of poverty and labor
had damaged Fanny's lungs.

Now seriously weak, Fanny was married in Lisbon and
soon after became pregnant. Fanny wrote to Wollstonecraft
and asked that she come to Lisbon to be with her at the
birth. Casting about her for the fare, Mary was offered
money by an anonymous friend. She always suspected the
source was the Reverend Richard Price.

When Fanny's invitation to visit her arrived, Mary
Wollstonecraft was indeed happy to go to Lisbon. The
school in Newington Green was in peril. The Wollstonecraft sisters were not always managing well and tended to be
quarrelsome. Mary found her sisters at times unreliable and
peevish; they found her occasionally headstrong and unsym-

pathetic. Besides, she missed Fanny, whom she idealized in her absence. Wollstonecraft found herself falling into self-pitying melancholy when she turned to her letter writing.

Her journey to Lisbon was revitalizing. The ship rolled and pitched with such force that most passengers on board took sick. When the wind was high, seawater poured in through the cabin windows. Not ill herself, Wollstonecraft nursed one invalid through the 13-day voyage, and, pleased at her own usefulness, reported to her sisters on her arrival in Lisbon that she was "tolerably well" and "calmer than I could have expected to be."

But any sense of well-being was short-lived. Fanny's baby was born prematurely and died soon afterward. Fanny was, wrote Wollstonecraft, in a "very low state," and was "so worn out that her recovery would be almost a resurrection." Fanny did not rally; and, as Wollstonecraft had anticipated, she died within days. The great friend of her girlhood was dead, the elegant, graceful figure Wollstonecraft had first admired at her drawing and sewing. Later, she wrote about Fanny, "The grave has closed over a dear friend, the friend of my youth; still she is present with me, and I hear her soft voice warbling as I stray over the heath."

Wollstonecraft stayed awhile in Lisbon. She was far away from home for the first time in her life, and there was much in this southern European capital to observe. The poverty in Lisbon, where roaming packs of dogs lunged for scraps of food, appalled her, as did the Roman Catholic Church's hold on the population. Wollstonecraft herself was raised as an Anglican, and she loved the pageantry of church ritual; indeed, she had thought Reverend Mr. Price's chapel was a bit too simple to inspire religious feeling. But in Lisbon she loathed the intolerance that required Hugh Skeys to bury Fanny, an Anglican, at night and in great secrecy. She was not impressed with the convents and monasteries, where, she thought, nuns and monks preferred to prepare for the next world rather than do good in this one.

The ship voyage home was even more disturbing. During the December voyage, her vessel encountered a French ship in danger of sinking. To Wollstonecraft's horror, the English captain of her ship refused to bring the foundering vessel's occupants on board, protesting that he did not have enough food for additional passengers. Wollstonecraft was outraged by such indifference to other people's suffering and told the captain she would bring him to swift justice in England if he failed to rescue the French ship's crew and passengers. She prevailed, and the refugees boarded the English ship. The journey continued uneventfully, and Wollstonecraft filed away the memory of the captain's selfishness for use in future writings.

At home, in the year 1786, the school in Newington Green continued to founder. Without their oldest sister's steadying presence, Everina and Eliza quarreled and drove away pupils. The paying boarder left in anger. Debts mounted and money to pay them dwindled. Wollstonecraft decided to abandon her school, and not only because money problems were overwhelming. The experiment of living with her sisters was coming to an end. She felt she had to help them settle somewhere, but she no longer was inclined to live with them. Whatever the world might offer her, it was time to meet it on her own. "I cannot guess what the girls will do," she wrote to George Blood. "My brother, I am sure, will not receive them and they are not calculated to struggle with the world." Ultimately, Everina did go back to Ned, and Eliza found a place in a boarding school. Meanwhile, friends of Mary's found work for her in Ireland as a governess to a titled family named Kingsborough. Although she believed that becoming a governess was more degrading than teaching school, as a governess she would have a small salary as well as time to consider how to launch herself again.

Some ideas were already brewing. Long ago Wollstonecraft had admired Jane Arden's prose style, and had modeled her own on it. Later, she admired Fanny's writing. But now her travels and new friendships had eclipsed Jane's and Fanny's knowledge of the world. She was the friend of liberal-minded intellectuals, such as the Reverend Mr. Price and the widow of the radical reformer and writer James Burgh, who greatly influenced the patriots who began the American Revolution. She had even met grand old Samuel Johnson, who had compiled the first dictionary of the English language. These were people who liked to encourage young women; they did not believe that young women, like children, should be seen only and not taken seriously. In fact, one such friend suggested she write to make money. Wollstonecraft took the proffered advice. In two short months, just back from Lisbon and while her school was disbanding and her sisters' futures were on her mind, she wrote her first published book, *Thoughts on the Education of Daughters.*

It was a good choice for a first book, since she herself had been educating other people's daughters for so many months. Other books giving advice on young women's education had been written, but those assumed that girls born into the aristocratic or middle classes should be trained primarily in traditional feminine skills, such as drawing and piano playing. There was, such older advice suggested, no need for girls to learn to use their minds. Most of these older writers did not believe girls had much of a mind to use. Increasingly, however, such opinions were considered antiquated and out of step with the progressive, reform-minded attitudes of the late 18th century. Moreover, the times were encouraging for young writers. Wollstonecraft was a young writer when writing itself was a young industry. As the century was ending, printing presses were pouring forth a flood of reading materials—books, newspapers, handbills, and essays. Much of this writing was calling for reform, challenging old notions of privilege. The British reading public had never been so well informed.

In *Thoughts,* Mary Wollstonecraft aired more progressive opinions. While other advice manuals indicated that girls must be taught only to submit to authority—and ultimately to the authority of a husband—Wollstonecraft insisted that they be raised to think for themselves. The minds of young girls should be shaped by attentive mothers and fathers, she claimed. In the spirit of the 17th-century political thinker John Locke, whose opinions shaped America's Declaration of Independence, Wollstonecraft suggested that a good and reasonable girl would flourish if she were taught by moral example.

Wollstonecraft wrote *Thoughts* hastily; already she was making plans to leave for Ireland. As she wrote, she wove her own memories, many of them painfully recent, into her work. Remembering her own parents' bad-tempered treatment of her, she urged mothers and fathers to talk with their children, to listen to their conversation, to answer their questions, and to be fair in their dealings with them. As she wrote of the hardship of young women who must make their own way in the world, she described her own experience in Bath as a paid companion: "It is impossible to enumerate the many hours of anguish such a person must spend. [She is] above the servants, yet considered by them a spy, and ever reminded of her inferiority when in conversation with the superiors." As for being a teacher, Wollstonecraft wrote that she is "only a kind of upper servant, who has more work than the menial ones."

Just months away from joining the Kingsboroughs in Ireland as a governess, Wollstonecraft continued to write her grim description of the alternative employments for women. "A governess to young ladies is equally disagreeable. . . . Ten to one," she wrote, "she will not meet a reasonable mother and the children will probably treat her with disrespect and insolence. . . . In the meantime, life glides away and the spirits with it."

Thoughts earned the new author some money. But, her debts were at least 10 times her earnings. Wollstonecraft gave her money to the Blood family who were returning to Ireland, but declined their invitation to join them. Instead, she intended to learn French to prepare for the lonely work of a governess at the Kingsboroughs. Yet life was not entirely gliding away. James Hewlitt, a clergyman and the friend who had encouraged her to write *Thoughts*, brought her to meet a publisher named Joseph Johnson, whose print shop was near St. Paul's Cathedral in the City of London. Many older men had admired and helped Mary Wollstonecraft in the past—Mr. Arden in Beverley, the Reverend Mr. Clare and Reverend Richard Price—but none would be so important as this publisher.

Joseph Johnson recognized talent and had a pleasant manner of fostering it. He was already publishing works by another woman, the learned liberal Anna Barbauld, who was interested in education. Increasingly, women were joining the vastly growing reading public. More women, he thought, could successfully write the stories and essays this book-loving public was eager to read. Mary Wollstonecraft sat and talked in his shop. When she left for Ireland, she carried in her head plans for books she meant to write.

With these hopes in mind, Wollstonecraft passed through the great gates of the Kingsboroughs' country house in the autumn of 1786. As she did so, her heart sank. In a letter she wrote later to Everina, she said that she felt that the gates of the French prison, the Bastille, were closing behind her. She had come to a vastly wealthy family. Their castle commanded a pleasant view of cloud-covered hills and sat upon extensive property that was under the wise governance of Lord Kingsborough. He was an enlightened landowner who had improved his estates and created industries for his tenants. But, Wollstonecraft was many miles from London, where she had learned to enjoy the company of witty, learned people interested in progressive politics and literature. She was also almost 200 miles from Dublin, and she worried that the Kingsboroughs would leave her and the children behind when they wintered in the city.

Moreover, there was Lady Kingsborough to please. Wollstonecraft had had a reassuring letter from her in which she

*Caroline, Lady
Kingsborough was
wife and mother of one
of the wealthiest
landowning families in
Ireland. Mary
Wollstonecraft was
both outraged and
amused by the vanity
of Lady Kingsborough
and her friends, notic-
ing how they "shame-
lessly" put on rouge
and could spend as
many as five hours a
day simply making up
their faces.*

confessed that her daughters had been so far only narrowly educated, stuffed with silly accomplishments, and lacking in substance. But in a letter to her sister Everina, Wollstonecraft worried that she might not be equal to teaching the girls the substance they lacked. Perhaps her well-meaning Newington Green friends had misrepresented her to her new employer. Then too Wollstonecraft knew she had come to Ireland in an inferior position. Always proud and sensitive, she was unwilling to admit any inferiority that was not moral or intellectual in nature. But, from childhood Mary had inherited some of her father's prejudices, and she was very conscious of social rank. She was prepared to be snubbed, to be condescended to, or worse, to be ignored. And she was prepared to be miserable.

Certainly, though, there was no ignoring Mary Wollstonecraft on her first day. In the drawing room, Wollstonecraft met a whole host of females: Lady Kingsborough, her stepmother and sisters, and too many other young women for Wollstonecraft to count. All of these women, it seemed to Wollstonecraft, were examining her with frank curiosity. Foremost among them was Lady Kingsborough, a strong-willed and volatile woman. From the beginning, Lady Kingsborough fascinated Wollstonecraft. She could not keep herself from studying her employer closely, even while she was quite emphatically denouncing her in letters to her sisters. Ultimately, Lady Kingsborough won an unenviable immortality at the hands of her governess when she became the model of all female folly, vanity, and dereliction of duty in the pages of *A Vindication of the Rights of Woman*.

Wollstonecraft took the measure of Lady Kingsborough on one occasion unremarkable to the Kingsboroughs, but heavy with significance to their new governess. Lying in bed one day,

Lady Kingsborough complained of a sore throat and consoled herself with her lapdogs, whom she fondled and teased in baby talk. Wollstonecraft called her behavior "absurd and ludicrous." "A fine lady is a new species to me of animal," she wrote Everina. The problem, as she saw it, was that such affection needed to be lavished on her children, not her dogs. And in this area, Lady Kingsborough, like Mary's own mother, was deficient.

Wollstonecraft was in charge of three daughters, the oldest of whom was 14. Mary found the young girl "sweet," with "a wonderful capacity," but with an intelligence that had yet to be trained. Contrary to what Lady Kingsborough had written to Wollstonecraft, these girls in fact had had some schooling. They understood several languages, which kept Mary busy at night studying French and Italian. The girls had been given "cartloads" of history to read, she wrote Everina, and were denied any novels, that new form of storytelling publishers like Joseph Johnson were dispensing to a reading-hungry public. Lady Kingsborough apparently shared a widespread concern that reading novels might be harmful to a young girl's moral character.

No one could be more concerned with character development than Mary Wollstonecraft. However, she felt that the training missing at the Kingsboroughs was the moral example of those close to the children. Their mother dispensed cold authority rather than affection, so that her daughters were quite frightened by her. The oldest daughter, Margaret, in particular shrank from her mother's company and had nervous bursts of temper. "That such a creature should be ruled with a rod of iron when tenderness would lead her anywhere" was an outrage to Wollstonecraft. As she wrote to Everina, recording her first impressions, she heard the music of a flute somewhere below and servants dancing elsewhere in the castle. She also could hear the Kingsborough family "diverting themselves." She belonged nowhere, she complained. "I only am melancholy and alone."

Loneliness and melancholy claimed her like a plague while she was with the Kingsboroughs, although the family was pleasant to her and their home was the center of a lively and important gentry life. Kingsborough castle hosted interesting guests. There were members of the Irish Parliament, for example, who debated Irish independence and Catholic emancipation through the disestablishment of the Church of England. If passed, disestablishment would end the Anglican Church's status as the official church of the realm.

In spite of the parties and the entertainments, in her own mind Wollstonecraft was always the governess in the home. If she were summoned to the drawing room after dinner, she was reluctant to go, haughty about accepting favors, and loath to leave once she had arrived. Moreover, she suspected that Lady Kingsborough was jealous of any attention that might be paid to her by attractive men. Wollstonecraft was also painfully conscious of her appearance. She would not—in fact, could not—spend any of her salary on hats or hair dressings, but she knew she made a sorry appearance in her old clothes. She had had to borrow money for the few garments she wore when she arrived. There was nothing left for luxuries. Once when Lady Kingsborough offered to buy her new clothing, Wollstonecraft coldly refused, and Lady Kingsborough was angry in response. Between the two strong-minded women sparks inevitably flew.

Money problems never left Mary Wollstonecraft. Embarrassed by heavy debts to Newington Green friends, she counted the months that would provide her with the salary that would allow her to put her creditors behind her. Meanwhile, Eliza and Everina wrote continually about their own misery. Wollstonecraft imagined sisterly reunions and suggested she might find other employments for them with the Kingsboroughs' help ("I am a GREAT favourite in the family," she confided), yet she was unable to help in any way. Anxious and alone, her melancholy took the form of physical weakness and disability. This was an old story; such affliction had occurred in Bath when Wollstonecraft was companion to Mrs. Dawson. Lady Kingsborough was alarmed enough to want to call in a doctor, but Wollstonecraft would have none of it.

Respite came when the family moved to Dublin in the winter, taking the girls and their governess. In Dublin was the "hurly-burly" of a city, she wrote to Everina, with rounds of social, cultural, and intellectual events to challenge her self-absorption. The Kingsboroughs lived in a great town house in a fashionable street, and Dublin society, which Wollstonecraft found friendly and hospitable, came to their door. She visited the theater, met the actors, and attended the assembly rooms where the most fashionable people played cards, danced, and listened to music.

In spite of her moods Wollstonecraft was a witty companion. Indeed, since she came to Ireland, she had been reading books widely, volumes sent by friends in Newington Green. She had read the newest edition of Shakespeare, a gift from George Blood, and seasoned her correspondence with quotes, usually the more melancholy lines, from *Hamlet*. She read the novels of Fanny Burney, one of the new women writers of the late 18th century; and the verses of William Cowper, one of the younger poets. She read Hugh Blair's famous and influential *Lectures on Rhetoric*, which helped to form her taste in literature. She read essays

In Ireland and across Britain, ladies and gentlemen customarily gathered in a drawing room after dinner to play cards, read, or doze in a chair all evening long. Mary Wollstonecraft wrote from Dublin, "I do not admire the Irish, and as to the great world and its frivolous ceremonies . . . they fatigue me—I thank Heaven that I wasn't so unfortunate as to be born a Lady of quality."

of moral philosophy, collections of sermons, and the great work of the French philosopher Jean-Jacques Rousseau, *Emile,* about the education of a young boy. The young governess was becoming a "bluestocking," one of those learned women who defied conventional expectations by educating themselves. This odd name perhaps suggested the indifference of these unconventional women to fashion. The name was taken from the Blue Stocking Society, a late 18th-century club of mostly literary women who wore stockings made of blue wool rather than the customary black silk.

Bluestocking or not, Wollstonecraft was writing. All along she corresponded with her publisher, Joseph Johnson, who encouraged her to write more books for money. In her letters to her sisters and friends, Wollstonecraft was used to chronicling the swings of her own moods with care and precision. As good as orphaned and without a private income, she had been making her own way in the world with great difficulty. Her life was the stuff of which stories were made. The growing reading public had an appetite for tales about heroines in great distress. Increasingly too, people had leisure time for reading, and the novel was a new literary form that the wisest and most respected London critics were willing to commend. Even the great Samuel Johnson, who wrote critical essays about Shakespeare, admired the novels of young Fanny Burney when, years earlier, she had acknowledged she was the anonymous author of the widely popular *Evelina*.

While she was with the Kingsboroughs, Wollstonecraft wrote her second book, a novel, *Mary, A Fiction*. With her first sentence, she began to mine the resources of her own life for the story she would tell. "Mary, the heroine of this fiction, was the daughter of Edward, who married Eliza. . . ." Eliza is a composite of Lady Kinsgsborough and her own mother, a fine lady who whispers fond phrases in French to her lapdogs and openly prefers her firstborn son to her daughter Mary. Like his real-life model, the fictional Edward drinks. Wollstonecraft chose not to write about the frightening memories when her father struck her mother while drunk, but she remembered and wrote about the mockery with which he greeted ideas of girls' receiving an education. She sets the fiction in a castle with nearby "cloud-capt" mountains, using the same phrase she had written to Everina when she first joined the Kingsboroughs. In *Mary* the young heroine is married off peremptorily by her parents to a man she does not love. Conveniently, the young husband travels to Europe to study. Mary is befriended by a young woman whose tubercular cough resembles Fanny's. She joins her friend in Lisbon, after stormy scenes at sea that recalled Wollstonecraft's own passage to Portugal years earlier.

There is no happy romance in Wollstonecraft's first novel, as there was none in her life. The only interesting young man is also seriously consumptive. He sadly wishes, "Could these arms shield thee from sorrow," to no avail. Dying, he tells Mary he cannot "afford thee an asylum from an unfeeling world." To contemporary tastes, the prose is hopelessly melo-dramatic. Mary "prayed wildly—and fervently—but attempt-ing to touch the lifeless hand—her head swum—she sunk."

Wollstonecraft's audience admired novels of feeling, with an appetite for expressions of sentiment that crested in the poetry of William Wordsworth, Percy Bysshe Shelley, and John Keats; the novels of Sir Walter Scott and Mrs. Radcliffe. *Mary* was not a well-written book. It was uneven in narrative and unconvincing in characterization. Johnson published it, but it was not widely read or profitable. More importantly, the work confirmed Wollstonecraft's conviction that she could be more in life than a governess.

While she was writing *Mary*, her time with the Kings-boroughs was drawing to a close. Not surprisingly Lady Kingsborough had grown a little intimidated by her governess, now known as the author of *Thoughts on the Education of Daughters*—or so Mary Wollstonecraft claimed when she wrote to Everina. A year after Wollstonecraft had first passed through the great gates of the Kingsborough home, her employer abruptly dismissed her, claiming that Margaret, her oldest daughter, had grown too fond of her governess. Wollstonecraft wrote to Everina that she was not surprised. "I long since imagined that my departure would be sudden," she explained. But in the uncertain months that lay ahead, she missed the affectionate companionship of the girls she had taught. She kept in contact with Margaret Kingsborough. Many years later Margaret wrote that only the intervention of Mary Wollstone-craft had rescued her from an unhappy childhood.

Although Wollstonecraft missed the little girls, she never regretted the vanished post of governess. When her books were published, she wrote teasingly to Eliza, "I hope you have not forgotten that I am an author." She herself had not forgotten; nor did she intend to be the author of only two books. Turning her direction south to London again, now 28 years old, she planned to ask her publisher for more employment. She would continue to write and make her own way in the world.

FROM *MARY, A FICTION*

Wollstonecraft poured all of the resentments she harbored against her often-violent father and her unaffectionate and indifferent mother into her autobiographical novel, Mary. *She suggested that the reasons for her own frequent unhappiness lay in her childhood and in the volatile personality she shared with her father.*

Her father always exclaimed against female acquirements, and was glad that his wife's indolence and ill health made her not trouble herself about them. She had besides another reason, she did not wish to have a fine tall girl brought forward into notice as her daughter; she still expected to recover, and figure away in the gay world. Her husband was very tyrannical and passionate; indeed so very easily irritated when inebriated, that Mary was continually in dread lest he should frighten her mother to death; her sickness called forth all Mary's tenderness, and exercised her compassion so continually, that it became more than a match for self-love, and was the governing propensity of her heart through life. She was violent in her temper; but she saw her father's faults, and would weep when obliged to compare his temper with her own.—She did more; artless prayers rose to Heaven for pardon, when she was conscious of having erred; and her contrition was so exceedingly painful, that she watched diligently the first movements of anger and impatience, to save herself this cruel remorse . . .

Her sensibility prompted her to search for an object to love; on earth it was not to be found: her mother had often disappointed her, and the apparent partiality she shewed to her brother gave her equisite pain— produced a kind of habitual melancholy, led her into a fondness for reading tales of woe, and made her almost realize the fictitious distress.

The bookseller Joseph Johnson lived above his shop in St. Paul's Churchyard in London. The city was the most densely populated area in England, with shopkeepers and their families living above their shops, and servants, apprentices, messengers, and porters tucked away under the roofs or in cellars.

VINDICATING THE RIGHTS OF WOMEN

". . . if I exert my talents in writing I may support myself
in a comfortable way. I am then going to be the first of a
new genus."

—Mary to Everina Wollstonecraft

In the shadow of the great dome of St. Paul's Cathedral,
Joseph Johnson's bookstore was the largest establishment in a
row of shops. The bookseller lived in rooms above the street
in a part of London that was burned down by the Great Fire
more than a hundred years earlier. The fire had begun in a
pie shop and blazed undiminished for four days until it leveled street after narrow street of timber and thatched houses,
destroying the old London town that had stood since the
Middle Ages. Around St. Paul's and the monument to the
Great Fire that stands nearby, the modern city of London
grew. "A city of more precious mold," wrote the poet John
Dryden about London rebuilt, "with silver paved, and all
divine with gold."

The gold in London's streets was passed over shop coun-
ters. In the book trade profits were likely if publishers chose
authors wisely, as Joseph Johnson did. More than simply a
tradesman, Johnson was a courageous patriot and a visionary,

Dissenter and political reformer Joseph Johnson published inexpensive books so that he might educate a broad portion of Britain's growing reading public. Wollstonecraft wrote to Johnson, "You are my only friend—the only person I am intimate with—I never had a father, or a brother— you have been both to me, ever since I knew you."

a man willing to take chances publishing essays that called for reform and revolution during dangerous times. Johnson opened his shop 20 years before Mary Wollstonecraft returned to London from Ireland to work for him. His bookshop was only a short walk from where the River Thames flowed past the ancient hall of Westminster, the shop itself surrounded by sellers of stationery, maps, prints, and music scores. Nearby on Fleet Street, Dr. Samuel Johnson had lived in an interior courtyard where the most famous poets, writers, and wits of the midcentury had visited him.

Joseph Johnson was a 50-year-old bachelor when Wollstonecraft became his protégée. Like the Reverend Price, the publisher was a Protestant dissenter, involved in promoting liberal reforms such as the repeal of the Test and Corporation Acts. These decrees required that officeholders, military officers, and students at the prestigious universities of Oxford and Cambridge all accept the tenets of the Anglican faith, acts that outraged religious nonconformists and fair-minded progressive reformers. These were people who argued for religious tolerance and the rights of individuals to practice their own beliefs without hindrance to the achievements their merits and hard work earned them.

When he met Mary Wollstonecraft, Johnson was already well known as the publisher of liberal tracts. More than 10 years earlier, when hostilities with the United States were erupting, he had printed the political essays of Benjamin Franklin. He became the publisher of the international patriot Thomas Paine soon afterward. Some of the most important thinkers and writers collected around Joseph Johnson. Among them were Joseph Priestley, discoverer of oxygen, chemist, and religious and political dissenter; the young poet and engraver William Blake; Henry Fuseli, the Swiss artist; Anna Barbauld, the writer; and William Godwin, dissenter and anarchist—political philosopher. Mary Wollstonecraft was joining some of the most interesting people in London—thinkers and writers who were creating the poetry, art, and political theory that shaped the character of the late 18th century.

Among them, Wollstonecraft was resolved to be independent, but she needed help. She wrote to Everina in the fall of l787, "Mr. Johnson whose uncommon kindness, I believe, has saved me from despair . . . assures me that if I exert my talents in writing I may support myself in a comfortable way. I am then going to be the first of a new genus. . . ." She reassured Everina that she hoped to have a home for her sisters when they had time to visit her, but she issued no invitations to share space permanently. Writing to George Blood, she explained, "I am determined on one thing, never to have my sisters live with me, my solitary manner of living would not suit them, nor could I pursue my studies if forced to conform."

With a new confidence in herself and her capacity for productive intellectual work, she told Everina, "You know I am not born to tread in the beaten track." She had arrived among people who did not accept religious beliefs or political traditions uncritically. Johnson and his circle argued for more widespread religious tolerance. They also argued for an expansion of the right to vote to include the growing classes of newly propertied industrial men in the great northern manufacturing cities of Leeds and Manchester. These hardworking, successful men

In its propaganda war against political reform, the English government at the end of the 18th century welcomed cartoons that mocked well-known religious dissenters and supporters of the French Revolution. Joseph Priestley, chemist, educator, and founder of Unitarianism, is depicted stepping on the Bible and clutching inflammatory political pamphlets.

DOCTOR PHLOGISTON,
The PRIESTLEY politician or the Political Priest.

were still unable to choose the parliamentary leaders who made the country's laws.

In the small house that Johnson found for her near Black-friars Bridge, a short walk from St. Paul's, Mary Wollstone-craft spent the busiest years of her life. True to his word, Johnson found work for her to do. She wrote book reviews for his journal, the *Analytical Review,* a task that brought the newest and most provocative writing across her desk. She translated works from French into English and studied German to expand her skills as a translator. She wrote a col-lection of instructive tales for young children titled *Original Stories,* and began, but left unfinished, a work of fiction called *Cave of Fancy.*

Work soothed and restored her. Writing about teaching children in *Original Stories* was more satisfying than the lonely work of being a governess, feeling patronized by parents. Wollstonecraft's fictional governess, Mrs. Mason, is stern and moralizing. She was quite unlike the kind of governess Wollstonecraft herself must have been to have won the affec-tion of the Kingsborough daughters. The stories struck the right note for more progressive parents in their suggestion that children's moral education might be approached rationally, by appealing to youngsters' native, though unformed, intelli-gence and goodness. Certainly such advice was more in keep-ing with the democratic political sympathies of Johnson's cir-cle than assuming young children were naturally driven by willful and selfish passions that needed to be beaten out of them with sticks. *Original Stories* sold well. They earned Johnson money, and launched Mary Wollstonecraft as one of a very few women in his circle of writers.

Writing helped keep her anxious, desperate moods at bay; but new to the game of pleasing critics, Wollstonecraft was aware that she wrote rapidly, often ungrammatically, and sometimes unclearly. Sending Johnson a chapter of a transla-tion, she said in her cover letter that she hoped he would not have "often to say—what does this mean?" Her letters to sis-

Look what a fine morning it is.—Insects Birds, & Animals, are all enjoying existence.

The poet and artist William Blake engraved this fron-tispiece illustration to Mary Wollstonecraft's Original Stories, *a collection of moral tales intended for the education of children. The* Original Stories *were a great success and convinced Wollstone-craft that she could earn her own way as a professional writer.*

ters and friends are torrents of prose, connected with infor-mal dashes, as if she were speaking, not writing.

Although she may have brooded over her grammar, she was growing confident about her opinions. As her relationship with Johnson changed, becoming more familiarly one of a col-league to another, she stood more confidently upon her own judgments and could remind him humorously that she was not to be brow-beaten. "If you do not like the manner in which I reviewed Dr. Johnson's essays on his wife," she wrote one day, "be it known unto you—I will not do it any other way—"

Joseph Johnson was Wollstonecraft's mentor and friend. Their relationship was warm but not romantic, although Wollstonecraft had confessed to a friend she preferred men past the "meridian" of life. By her own accounts, he gave her the gentle nurturing of her talent that she might have had from a better father or older brother. When she needed money, as she did so frequently, he gave her advances.

As always, her financial affairs were a tangle of borrowing and lending. She was neither embarrassed by borrowing nor self-satisfied by lending. Money was simply a means of getting on with the work of life, as when, just established in London, she sent Everina to Paris to learn French. Caring too much about money, she suggested to Johnson, was a vulgar preoccupation of shopkeepers. Johnson himself, she told him, as she borrowed money from him, was above such worries.

Although she would not live with her sisters or her brothers, her home was theirs on their holidays. She assumed responsibility for their livelihoods and constantly looked out for their advancement. Writing to friends, she asked for better teaching posts for her sisters. She sent James to school to train as a naval officer and looked for a career for young Charles in the United States. With Johnson's help, Mary acted as the head of the family, displacing Ned. She also took over the management of her father's business affairs, since Edward Wollstonecraft was now a gaunt and haggard drunk, his health ruined.

From London, Wollstonecraft even continued to manage the affairs of the Blood family. One letter to George Blood offers a glimpse into the labyrinth of financial arrangements she superintended. In it Wollstonecraft asks that he urge his father to send her money to defray expenses of a job she had found for one of his daughters. In that way Wollstonecraft could then repay a Mrs. Fitzgerald, from whom she had borrowed money to give to Bess Delaney, another Blood family friend. Somehow Mary kept this tangle of indebtedness in her head, as she sent out for books and paper, mended her pens, wrote her essays, and hurried to finish her work while the young boy sent by the printer to collect pages of manuscript waited at the door.

When she was lonely and unhappy, or when she simply wanted to put down her pen and papers to talk, she walked across Blackfriars Bridge to Johnson's rooms above his shop. Johnson remembered that she took this walk many afternoons and evenings. She made a striking impression: Her hair was not carefully combed, her dress was simple and not always tidy. She came from barely furnished rooms that had been put together with little money or interest in comfort or luxury. She was similarly uninterested in her appearance. But whatever plainness there was in her clothing, there was nothing shy about her presence. Anyone sitting at Johnson's instantly knew what she was feeling or thinking. She was outspoken and passionate about what she believed. Johnson later wrote that if she arrived troubled, she poured forth all her woes to her friends, and then returned home calm.

Joseph Johnson was a popular host. In the tradition of booksellers, he gave weekly dinner parties, where the bright and energetic reformers whom he was publishing met and spiritedly debated the great political questions of their day. Johnson put boiled cod, roasted veal, vegetables, and rice pudding in front of them; and while his guests ate their dinners, their opinions flew rapidly back and forth. These soirees were famously entertaining, with the genial publisher presiding over the roar of talk. Anna Barbauld wrote that the conversation at Johnson's dinners moved so quickly, she was startled to discover that it was well past midnight when everyone finally left for home.

In 1789 Johnson's dinner guests had much to discuss. In July a Parisian mob stormed the Bastille, and in October the king and queen, who had thought they reigned with the approval of God, were forced to leave their splendid country palace at Versailles for Paris. There, they watched their power erode. In place of the monarchy that had ruled for centuries, the patriots in France declared a Republic and raised the banner of "the rights of man." All over Europe thrones shook from the

On July 14, 1789, crowds of Parisians, alarmed by the king's troops gathered outside the city, marched to the old stronghold of the Bastille and demanded arms from the prison's governor. When he refused, the crowd turned into an angry mob and stormed the prison, murdering soldiers, the prison governor, and the mayor of Paris, whose heads they mounted on pikes and paraded around the city.

upheaval. Truly, an epoch had come to an end, and the age of republicanism and democracy was beginning. The divine right of kings, the centuries-old belief that heaven itself ordained that a king should rule, was shattered. Also ended were the inherited privileges of an aristocracy. Dukes, counts, barons, and their ladies were now mere citizens. Equality was the watchword on everyone's lips. "Bliss was it in that dawn to be alive," said the poet William Wordsworth "But to be young was very heaven."

British intellectuals joyfully embraced the news from France. In 1789 the streets of Paris were not yet running with blood. The king and queen, although little more than prisoners, were still alive; and the Reign of Terror, which would in a few short years send patriots to the guillotine alongside aristocrats, had not yet begun. Small wonder that so many progressive thinkers in Britain were exultant. British reformers had been laboring for years to end the power and privilege of an aristocracy that ruled only because of an accident of birth. Now they rejoiced that across the Channel, French patriots were abolishing the antiquated political and economic privileges of their ruling class.

Nor was it simply the throne and the nobility whose powers were ending. In England nonconforming Protestants, whose rights were limited because of their religious beliefs, applauded news that in France a state church finally was dismantled and a new religion of reason had replaced the arbitrary privilege given to one religion alone. Such men as the Reverend Richard Price, Wollstonecraft's old friend from Newington Green, believed that at last a people had thrown off their oppressive yoke and were free to build a better society.

Several months after the Bastille was stormed Mr. Price delivered a sermon that set off a political firestorm. He was asked to deliver an address to the Revolution Society. This organization annually celebrated the English Settlement of 1688, which had greatly reduced the power of the British monarchy and strengthened that of Parliament. When Reverend Price rose to his feet that day, he congratulated the French National Assembly for bringing civil and religious liberty to France. As he continued to speak, however, he touched on themes that others beyond the doors of the Revolution Society regarded with alarm. Dr. Price spoke about a person's being a citizen of the world, rather than having allegiance to only one particular place. He explained the doctrine of perfectibility, the belief that a society could be organized along principles of justice and goodness so that all citizens would have happy lives.

"What an eventful period is this!" said Price that day. "I am thankful that I have lived to see it. . . . I have lived to see the

Smelling out a Rat;— or The Atheistical-Revolutionist disturbed in his Midnight Calculations.

James Gillray's political cartoon shows the Rev. Richard Price surprised at his desk by the looming figure of the conservative parliamentary leader Edmund Burke. Burke, holding cross and crown, had just written Reflections on the Revolution in France, *defending church and monarchy against assaults by political reformers and religious dissenters like Price.*

rights of man better understood than ever. . . . and now methinks I see the ardour of liberty catching and spreading, a general amendment beginning in human affairs, the dominion of kings changed for the dominion of laws, and the dominion of priests giving way to the dominion of reason and conscience."

These were ideas that had animated the American Revolution in 1776, which proclaimed the "inalienable rights" of men to "life, liberty, and the pursuit of happiness." Many reform-minded Britons had applauded the American Revolution, among them Edmund Burke, the British parliamentary leader. Burke believed that the American patriots—men like Thomas Jefferson, Benjamin Franklin, and John Adams—were simply demanding the ancient civil liberties of all British peoples. But he recoiled with horror from the news in France. He believed that societies flourished if they protected their traditions. To Burke the old aristocratic families of Britain were like the great oak trees with roots deep in British soil, splendid and vital.

When the clergyman's words were circulated through-out London, it seemed to men like Burke that Price wanted to dig up those ancient trees, level the ground in which they grew, and build something new. Whatever kind of society Price built, worried Burke, would have no founda-tion, no roots, no soundness, no splendor. To him the social experimentation in Paris was evil, conducted by zealots with no respect for tradition or continuity.

In November 1790, after angrily writing and revising all year, Burke published his *Reflections on the Revolution in France,* his much-anticipated response to Price. In it he pre-dicted chaos and terror in France, denying the doctrine of perfectibility and its companion assumption: that equal rights belong to all men. "This new and hitherto-unheard of, bill of rights though made in the name of the whole people, belongs to those gentlemen and their faction only," wrote Burke, meaning Price and the group of men around Joseph Johnson. "The body of the people of England have no share in it. They utterly disclaim it." Burke's response was so widely sought that printers hastily arranged for more copies to be issued than they had originally planned. The liberal community of dissenters and reformers— among them Wollstonecraft—received Burke's challenge and prepared themselves to reply.

Thomas Paine, political pamphleteer, galvanized American opinion on the side of independence early in 1776. Paine was self-educated and from humble origins, occa-sionally drunk and vulgar, offending President John Adams, who called Paine "a mongrel between pig and puppy."

Mary Wollstonecraft was 30 years old when the Bastille was overrun and the French Revolution began. She was living the best years of her young life. Now beyond the despondency and paralyzing self-doubt of her early years, she knew herself as a capable thinker and writer, someone who might respond to the challenge Burke had raised. When she lost confidence, she knew how to rally. One evening in the middle of the frenzy of writing a response to Burke, Wollstone-craft found herself unable to continue. Suddenly she was weary of the project. As she so often did, she made her way to Johnson's home, where she poured forth her troubles. No problem at all, he reassured her. They would destroy all the pages that were printed already and she could lay aside her work. Wollstonecraft returned home puzzled and disturbed by his response. She had expected reproach rather than sympathy. With new resolve, she set about her work until it was done. Mary Wollstonecraft was ready to take center stage in a political debate that convulsed the English-speaking world.

Her essay, *A Vindication of the Rights of Men,* was one of the first responses to Burke to go into print. There would ultimately be others, including Thomas Paine's important pamphlet, *The Rights of Man.* Again Wollstonecraft wrote hastily, as if in the first rush of angry indignation. In fact, Johnson printed each page of the manuscript as she finished it. So eager was he to publish the first volley in the skirmish that followed, he did not wait for the whole essay to be completed.

Burke's attack on Wollstonecraft's old mentor Richard Price had offended her. Although at 62 Burke was hardly a young man, Wollstonecraft imagined Price at 68 to have arrived at a venerable old age. She complained that Burke treated the clergyman with "indecent familiarity and supercilious contempt," rather than being respectful of Price's white hair and distinguished years. Still, *A Vindication of the Rights of Men* is more than a defense of Price. Wollstonecraft's essay is a showpiece of her developing social and political theories. Writing her response to Burke, Wollstonecraft lays claim for the first time to a systematic vision of social welfare based on a belief that men and women are born with a capacity to be reasonable, able to learn to live ethically and justly with each other. Wollstonecraft argued that, because this capacity to reason is given by God, it is indeed a right. The rights that Burke found ludicrous, Wollstonecraft claimed were the foundations of a good society. Whereas Burke searched for a good society in the traditions inherited from the past, Wollstonecraft believed a better society lay ahead.

All of Wollstonecraft's life and learning helped frame this first effort at political writing. Her schooling had been in the pews of Price's chapel in Newington Green, where she had learned to believe in progress, and at Johnson's dinner table, where she had learned to believe in human rights. With ideas about progress and human rights, she could make sense of her own experience in Beverley, Bath, Newington Green, and Dublin.

Responding to Burke, Wollstonecraft assailed the idols she believed he served: inherited property and traditional privileges. The unmerited possession of property, she argued in her essay, destroyed the human capacity to be rational, and therefore, virtuous. Certainly her father, who had not earned his bread through honest work, had become morally weak and corrupt, thereby spoiling any chance of happiness for his family. Her brother Ned, who as his father's oldest son had inherited all that remained of their grandfather's fortune, was indifferent to his brothers' and sisters' welfare. Burke, according to Wollstonecraft, was dazzled by property. He was the "adorer of the golden image which power has set up." Instead, she argued, "the only security of property is the right a man has to enjoy the acquisition which his talent and industry have acquired."

In his *Reflections,* Wollstonecraft wrote, Burke is so concerned about the troubles of the queen of France, around whom he thought chivalrous gentlemen should have rallied, that he could not hear the distress of the "many industrious mothers, whose helpmates have been torn from them, and the hungry cry of helpless babies." Burke's respect for tradition was "a servile reverence for antiquity." By the same misguided logic of respecting all of the practices of the past, insisted Wollstonecraft, even the horrific slave trade should never be abolished.

As Wollstonecraft warmed to her argument, she found reason to dislike more than Burke's *Reflections on the French Revolution.* In an earlier important essay on literary taste, he had described women in terms Wollstonecraft found insulting and dangerous. Women were beautiful, Burke had suggested, because they were weaker than men. Pausing in her response to his *Reflections* in order to recall his earlier essay, Wollstonecraft asked if Burke believed women had no need at all to develop their minds. Her own father had mocked the idea of a girl's being given a serious education. Men like Burke believed a woman's purpose was to be beautiful and to please men.

In questioning Burke, Wollstonecraft was laying the groundwork for the essay she would soon begin—*A Vindication of the Rights of Woman*. As she wrote her response to Burke, she left unanswered the question of whether she was addressing *human* rights or simply *men's* rights. The call issued from France had been only about the "rights of men." The American Declaration of Independence had stated merely that "all men are created equal." Very few people believed that women were included in those pronouncements. In fact, a long and respected tradition supported by the Bible pro-claimed the opposite: that women were physically and men-tally inferior to men and were divinely intended to be so. In Genesis, the first book of the Bible, Adam says of Eve, "This is now bone of my bones, and flesh of my flesh: she shall be called Woman, because she was taken out of man." Corinthians continues: "For the man is not of the woman; but the woman of the man. Neither was the man created for the woman but the woman for the man." St. Paul had said plainly, "Wives submit to your husbands."

Some few decades before Mary Wollstonecraft wrote, the force of this assumption of female inferiority was so wide-spread in English law that the jurist Sir William Blackstone gave it precise language. Women are less capable than men, he argued in his influential codification of English common law in 1758. Therefore they were quite properly under the governance of their male relations, even when they were fully grown. Having announced this subordinate status for women, Sir Blackstone proclaimed what became known as their civil "death." He suggested that as far as the state was concerned, in order to protect the rights of property, women did not exist. Rather than control their own money, women

must accept that their wealth would pass into the hands of their husbands or their sons. They could not enter into business contracts or own property. They were in short helpless: victims of fortune hunters to whom their father's wealth might pass, or victims of brutes who might, with the right of a husband, legally beat or rape them.

No one had vindicated the rights of women, although occasionally some voices had been raised. In Britain, late in the 17th century, the essayist Mary Astell had argued for women's education. More recently, historian and Bluestocking Catharine Macaulay, whose work Wollstonecraft reviewed and admired, insisted women could not become fully moral human beings if they were not educated. Thomas Paine also had spoken out for women's rights, as had the French revolutionary playwright Olympe de Gouges. Then too there had been the many women learning and writing as the 18th century continued. Earlier in the century, the poet and satirist Jonathan Swift had mocked the "furniture of a woman's mind," laughing about how she never holds her tongue a minute, "while all she prates has nothing in it." By century's end, however, many obviously intelligent and talented women were visible. The novelist Fanny Burney, the classical scholar Elizabeth Carter, the historian Catharine Macaulay, the dissenter and essayist Anna Barbauld, and the political author Hannah More were highly respected writers.

Those learned English women called "blue-stockings" are represented here as muses in the Temple of Apollo, god of sun and music. Mary Wollstonecraft particularly esteemed the historian Catherine Macaulay (seated at the base of the statue). Her 1790 Letters on Education *urged equal academic study and physical exercise for women and men.*

To be sure, not all of them supported the idea of formal education for women. In fact, despite her progressive politics, Anna Barbauld was opposed to founding a girls' school. Hannah More thought the idea of women's rights was quite ridiculous; and when Wollstonecraft's essay was published, she refused to read it. Nevertheless, precisely because serious and intelligent women were contributing to the intellectual, literary, and political life of England, they were undermining the long-standing assumption of women's intellectual inferiority.

The time was ripe for a defense of women's rights. Those men and women who believed in the French Revolution and the Enlightenment argued that the light of reason would dispel the mists of ignorance and superstition that had, until now, slowed the progress of societies. Such an argument, yet to be written, must destroy the logic by which women were excluded from the call for liberty. Wollstonecraft was ready to write this work. Her response to Burke had sold out so quickly that Johnson had rushed a second edition into print. She had followed custom and published the first edition anonymously, but encouraged by the popular reception of her work, she allowed the second edition to bear her name. Proudly, she sent the Reverend Mr. Price a signed copy of her work, and received his pleased reply, saying he had known since her teaching days at Newington Green that she was a talented woman. Suddenly the name Mary Wollstonecraft was being passed around London, and she found herself acclaimed as a worthy player in the political crossfire between Burke and his detractors.

Late in 1791 Wollstonecraft sat down to write *A Vindication of the Rights of Woman*. Her entire life had prepared her to make this argument, and she had never been so confident about defending her ideas. Only recently she had been to a dinner at Johnson's, where she was invited to meet the celebrated Thomas Paine. The fiery radical patriot had sat quietly that night, but Wollstonecraft had argued heatedly with another dinner guest, the anarchist writer William Godwin.

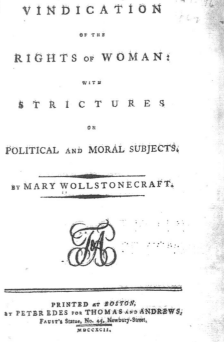

VINDICATION

OF THE

RIGHTS OF WOMAN:

WITH

STRICTURES

ON

POLITICAL AND MORAL SUBJECTS.

BY MARY WOLLSTONECRAFT.

PRINTED AT BOSTON,
BY PETER EDES FOR THOMAS AND ANDREWS,
FAUST's Statue, No. 45, Newbury-Street,
MDCCXCII.

Political debating was her element. She wrote rapidly, and again the young boy working for Johnson waited at her doorstep for each page of manuscript as it was completed. In six weeks, the essay was written. With her pen, Wollstonecraft launched the modern feminist debate on the rights of women.

At the outset Wollstonecraft targeted her argument precisely. She was interested, she claimed, in the moral rehabilitation of middle-class women, women whom she believed to be in a "natural" state: neither corrupted by the vanities of aristocratic life nor overwhelmed by the heavy cares of poverty. Here were reasonable, moral, and admirable women who might be useful to society. Yet they were, she wrote, often foolish, vain, and ignorant, an embarrassment to their sex, a brake on the forward movement of society rather than assisting its continual improvement.

Wollstonecraft believed that women were not naturally the idle fools they had too often become. *A Vindication of the Rights of Woman* explains that a "false system of education" is

Susan B. Anthony, leader of the women's movement for the vote in America, inscribed this copy of Wollstonecraft's Vindication, *which she called "the earliest work for women's right to equality of rights ever penned by a woman." Anthony, citing Ralph Waldo Emerson, 19th-century American essayist, wrote, "'a troublesome discontent is the first step toward progress,' and here in 1792 we have the first step—I think."*

responsible for the sorry condition of middle-class women. For example, "Women are told from infancy and taught by the example of their mothers" that if they appear weak, mild mannered, and obedient, they would find a man to protect them. If they were so fortunate as to be beautiful, they needed no other talents "for at least twenty years of their lives."

Not only did their education encourage girls to be submissive and ignorant, their upbringing actually nurtured bodily weakness. Girls were kept inside, fumed Wollstonecraft, listening to idle chatter, helping their mothers dress, and playing with dolls. Meanwhile boys "frolic in the open air." Nor would these girls' mothers set a very good example. Remembering Lady Kingsborough, Wollstonecraft remarked acidly, "I once knew a weak woman of fashion, who was more than commonly proud of her delicacy and sensibility. She thought a distinguishing taste and puny appetite the height of all human perfections, and acted accordingly." Alas, with the "intellectual world shut against them," girls arrived at womanhood "decked with artificial graces. . . . How grossly do they insult us," Wollstonecraft claimed, "who thus advise us only to render ourselves gentle, domestic brutes."

Wollstonecraft recognized the weighty tradition that authorized treating women like grown-up children, a tradition canonized by the Bible and codified in civil law. Surely, she protested, "the divine right of husbands may be contested in this enlightened age like the divine right of kings." The problem was, men did not understand that, like themselves, women are "human creatures" who should acquire "human" virtues, such as the virtue of living according to innate reason. Wollstonecraft would not accept that a God would create one rule of morality for men and another for women. "For man and woman . . . truth must be the same," she insisted. The rule that governed both man and woman was the necessity to live according to reason and develop one's mind.

Wollstonecraft believed that if girls were educated to become rational women, they in turn would become rational mothers, women who would educate their children well and contribute to the improvement of society. Importantly, she did not believe such wholesale social improvement would ever arise from the reform of individual women, because few individuals can resist the weight of social prejudices, traditions, and practices. "Men and women must be educated in a great degree, by the opinions and manners of the society they live in," she conceded. Until society is "differently constituted," she warned, "much cannot be expected from education."

Wollstonecraft thus challenged the apparatus of law itself, which reduced middle-class women to economic dependence on men. Arguing against Blackstone's codification of English common law, she said that a woman "must have a civil existence in the state." "She must not be dependent on her husband's bounty for her subsistence during her life, or support after his death." Wollstonecraft had not forgotten her mother's helplessness and her sisters' dependency on their brother. However, she learned to locate the source of her own personal problems in political and economic traditions. At last the personal trials of Edward Wollstonecraft's daughter found general language in public debate.

Wollstonecraft also challenged the system of education. By long-standing practice, schools provided a serious curriculum for boys, training in the classical languages of Latin and Greek, but only a smattering of "accomplishments" for girls, some French, some drawing, some English. Indeed Wollstonecraft and her sisters had taught little else at their Newington Green school. Wollstonecraft loathed as well the popular custom of packing children off to boarding schools, where she believed they learned one another's bad habits without any of the redeeming character of family life. Instead, she argued for a national and coeducational system of day schools for all children. She urged that girls study history and politics along with boys, and that both sexes be given ample time to exercise in the open air in order to develop robust bodies alongside intelligent minds.

WOLLSTONECRAFT'S CALL TO ARMS

In her argument for women's rights in A Vindication of the Rights of Woman, *Wollstonecraft reminded her reform-minded readers that the same logic opposing the rule of kings must oppose the rule of men over women. Wollstonecraft scornfully denied that a just God would injure half the human race by making them intellectually unequal to the other half.*

Let not men then in the pride of power, use the same arguments that tyrannic kings and venal ministers have used, and fallaciously assert that woman ought to be subjected because she has always been so. But, when man, governed by reasonable laws, enjoys his natural freedom, let him despise woman, if she do not share it with him; and, till that glorious period arrives, in descanting on the folly of the sex, let him not overlook his own . . .

It is time to effect a revolution in female manners—time to restore to them their lost dignity—and make them, as part of the human species, labour by reforming themselves to reform the world. It is time to separate unchangeable morals from local manners. If men be demigods, why let us serve them! And if the dignity of the female soul be as disputable as that of animals . . . they are surely of all creatures the most miserable! and, bent beneath the iron hand of destiny, must submit to be a "fair defect" in creation. But to justify the ways of Providence respecting them, by pointing out some irrefragable reason for thus making such a large portion of mankind accountable and not accountable, would puzzle the subtilest casuist.

Wollstonecraft also suggested more employments be opened up to women. Why should women not study healing, she asked, and become physicians? Why should they not operate places of business? Ultimately, she argued, women should vote, as well as all men. "It is time to effect a revolution in female manners," she proclaimed, "time to restore to them their lost dignity—and make them, as a part of the human species, labour, by reforming themselves to reform the world."

No one who read her essay could possibly be indifferent to her brave, tempestuous, and groundbreaking argument. Some intellectual and progressive women thought it "wonderful," "oftener right than wrong," "sensible and just." Others were impressed but startled at the widespread alteration Wollstonecraft urged in women's condition. One young American woman wrote, "She speaks my mind, [but] I am not for quite so much independence." Certainly many more readers were shocked and alarmed by the assault on tradition and law that Wollstonecraft's essay waged.

Many of the outraged responses were crafted by a massive propaganda campaign led by the British government, intended to depict any calls for reform as the beginnings of chaos and disorder, leading to bloodshed and terror. By 1793 the English government was truly alarmed by the influence of the French Revolution on political unrest at home. With the revolution raging across the Channel, the reform movement in England acquired a broader base of popular support than merely dissenting ministers such as Richard Price and Joseph Priestley. Large, ominous gatherings of tradesmen, mechanics, and shopkeepers were supporting the French revolutionaries and calling for reform in Parliament. Revolutionary clubs were forming all across England, and Joseph Johnson was publishing political pamphlets, such as American patriot Joel Barlow's *Advice to the Privileged Orders,* which echoed the sentiments of Thomas Paine's *The Rights of Man.*

A year after Wollstonecraft's *Vindication* was published, British Prime Minister William Pitt's government took stock of this alarming mood of discontent and fought back. Thomas Paine himself was threatened with imprisonment and fled to Paris. Responses to the *Vindication* echoed this political hysteria. The essayist Horace Walpole called Wollstonecraft "a hyena in petticoats," implying that a woman who argues for the rights of her sex is as unnatural and ridiculous as that screeching animal dressed up in lace. A critic writing for a political review wrote, "For Mary verily would wear the breeches/God help poor silly men from such usurping b . . . . . s." Even the Wollstonecraft sisters, working quietly at their teaching posts, were the objects of curious and apprehensive attention. Eliza, a governess near Pembroke, found that her employers would rise and leave the room if she opened her mouth about politics. She wrote to Everina, who lived nearby, that villagers burned Thomas Paine in effigy and threatened as well "to immortalize Miss Wollstonecraft in the like manner." Mary Wollstonecraft was suddenly famous, admired and abused in one breath, but also read and discussed in England, across the Channel in France, across the ocean in America. Her essay went into a second edition in a year and was translated into French and German.

As author of this revolutionary essay, Wollstonecraft had every reason to be exultant, but in the months following the frenzy of composition, her spirits sank. There were, of course, the inevitable cares of her family: the continuing need to find employment for her sisters and brothers, and the worry that one day the financial support of her father would wholly descend on her own shoulders. But other, more disturbing concerns were plaguing her.

At 33 years old, Mary Wollstonecraft was singularly alone. She had Johnson's circle of wits, scholars, and patriots; but since girlhood, she sought profound and passionate attachments with particular friends. She had not yet discovered love between two like-minded persons who preferred each other to the rest of the world.

One or two candidates had indeed presented themselves. Shortly after she had arrived in London, an acquaintance that she had met at Johnson's appeared at her rooms to offer her his hand. The man had been moved by Wollstonecraft's poverty and offered to provide her with the financial security of marriage to a person of property. Wollstonecraft was outraged and wrote to Johnson in wrathful pique. No matter how desperate her economic misfortune, she would not marry simply to relieve it. How dare Johnson encourage anyone to believe otherwise? Later, she wrote proudly to her sisters that she had refused an offer that would have ended her poverty. No vice was as clear to her as marrying for money. She prized romantic love too keenly as a noble sentiment. To her it was a perfect understanding and expansion of two human souls. In her letters and novels she always sang the praises of the claims of the heart.

Or did she prize this love? Strangely, her essay, *A Vindication of the Rights of Woman,* dismisses romantic love. It would be better, argued Wollstonecraft in these pages, if a husband and wife did not love each other long after marriage. Let those romantic passions cool, and let a serene friendship replace them, a friendship based on respect for each other's wisdom and goodness. A household based on the friendship between parents would be much happier. "Love," she warned, is a "stalking mischief."

In fact, love was making mischief for Wollstonecraft even as she was writing the *Vindication.* Willingly or no, she had fallen in love with Henry Fuseli, the Swiss painter she had met at Johnson's—and a married man. Certainly much about Fuseli would have attracted her. He was a good deal older than she, and by all accounts brilliant. A scholar, artist, and wit, Fuseli was also a political liberal; and his art was daring. He was used to commanding attention. Someone called his humor "a formidable force of gunnery." Wollstonecraft regarded Fuseli's marriage as a misfortune. She referred to this relationship only as a "peculiar circumstance," although a painfully limiting one. So long as

Fuseli lived, she told Eliza, she would always have an indulgent, warm friend, but a friend she could not visit as frequently or have nearby as often as she would like. In his turn, Fuseli confided to friends that Wollstonecraft with her untidy hair and plain clothes was a "philosophic sloven," while the women he painted and the woman he married were notable beauties.

Wollstonecraft had railed against female vanity, but her friends were noticing subtle transformations. Her living quarters became less Spartan, more comfortable. She moved from simple rooms near Johnson's to a larger house in Store Street, behind the British Museum in north London, a neighborhood preferred by artists. In fact, Fuseli lived within easy walking distance. The Store Street lodgings were more completely furnished, although when the French politician Talleyrand visited her there, eager to meet the author of the *Vindication of the Rights of Woman,* she served him wine in cracked teacups.

At the same time Wollstonecraft began to pay attention to her dress. Yet the appearance she made cannot be described simply. Portraits of her done during this period show contradictory moods, suggesting vibrancy in her character that could not be captured in one sitting. One unknown artist painted her as stern, almost fearsome, while another saw her as soft and contemplative. One man wrote, "Mary was without being a dazzling beauty, yet of a charming grace. Her face, so full of expression, presented a style of beauty beyond that of merely regular features. There was enchantment in her glance, her voice, and her movements."

Whatever the attraction of Wollstonecraft for Fuseli, he was unwilling to break up his household on her behalf. Meanwhile, the weary complaint of loneliness Mary had made to Eliza had become unendurable for her. Because he was married, Fuseli was too seldom in her company. For a short while, in the spring after the *Vindication* was published, Wollstonecraft hoped to travel to France with the Fuselis and Johnson. Her essay had been printed, translated, and praised in Paris, and she looked forward to meeting the political and literary luminaries there who knew her work. But the trip, as planned, did not take place. Johnson was not well, and good reasons discouraged the Fuselis from keeping their travel date.

Impetuously, Wollstonecraft confronted Mrs. Fuseli and made an astounding proposal that she join their household. Sophia Fuseli may have been willing to ignore the determined admiration the author of *A Vindication of the Rights of Woman* had conceived for her husband, but she was unwilling to share her home with her. Sophia Fuseli was outraged, but Wollstonecraft was adamant that her desire was moral and urgent. She believed that her romantic interest in Henry Fuseli was founded in rationality as well as sentiment. Writing later to Fuseli's wife, Wollstonecraft explained that her proposal "arises from the sincere affection which I have for your husband, for I find that I cannot live without the satisfaction of seeing and conversing with him daily." To Fuseli himself she wrote, "If I thought my passion criminal, I would conquer it, or die in the attempt. For immodesty, in my eyes, is ugliness; my soul turns with disgust from pleasure tricked out in charms which shun the light of heaven."

Henry Fuseli dropped from sight while the two women negotiated. The confrontation was brief. Sophia Fuseli registered her horror and Wollstonecraft, humiliated, fled the field. In the wake of this episode, London was unendurable. The knot of friends around Fuseli was too close and small to allow the embarrassment to be buried and forgotten. Wollstonecraft complained to Johnson that she was not well. Her nerves were shattered, she was sleeping badly, and she was restless. "There is certainly a great defect in my mind," she wrote, "— my wayward heart creates its own misery."

Her traveling companions had vanished, but France remained. There, she was celebrated as a famous author. There, patriots were lifting the lamp of reason to expel privilege and corruption. Writing to a friend, Wollstonecraft announced her departure. Just before Christmas in 1792, she arrived in Paris to see the revolution at firsthand.

CHAPTER

5

REVOLUTION AND ROMANCE IN PARIS

When Mary Wollstonecraft arrived in Paris in December 1792, she came to a city in crisis. King Louis XVI was in prison and about to be tried for treason against the French people. The price of bread had risen dramatically, and the working class was hungry and angry. Worse, the people who were orchestrating the Revolution were divided among themselves, uncertain about the violence that was unleashed, uncertain how to regulate the desperate French economy. France was the spiritual home of the European Enlightenment, home of the progressive thinkers called the philosophes, including satirist and philosopher Voltaire and the social theorist Jean-Jacques Rousseau. These men criticized dogmatic religion in the name of tolerance and envisioned a future of unlimited progress. Now France was showing Europe how to make a republic out of a monarchy—but progress was uneven and often bloody.

Paris itself looked much as it always had. To be sure, lamps now lit the streets, and the ancient cemeteries had been cleared from the city center. But the splendid cathedrals of Nôtre Dame and Sainte-Chapelle still dominated the maze of cobblestone streets, and the eight feudal towers and 80-foot

During the revolutionary years in France informal associations of citizens sprang up to read about the rights of man, write manifestos of their own, or, as in the case of this women's club, to donate jewelry to the Revolution.

walls of the Bastille were not yet leveled. As always, the fish-wives clustered in the central markets, and the jewelers and goldsmiths worked along the quays or in the arcades. Nine out of 10 Parisians still lived in crowded courtyards and alleys, with master craftsmen and journeyman apprentices living and working together in boardinghouses and old tenements.

Wollstonecraft was not impressed at first. The streets were dirty, often running with sewage, and without pavements for walking. Moreover, in the freezing winter Paris was difficult and expensive to cross when she had to hire a coach. She was also headachy and in the throes of a cold she had caught while traveling. The unfamiliar French language coursed by her as a stream of "flying words," and when she had to speak, she was suddenly bashful, with all her "fine French phrases" taking flight as well. Later, she wrote home to a friend that she said "oui oui" to most questions until someone warned her that she was perhaps saying "yes" when she meant otherwise.

Happily, she was staying at a most "excellent" and "comfortable" home, although it was also an empty one. Her hostess, Aline Fillietaz, was the daughter of the woman who ran the school in Putney where her sisters taught. Since Monsieur and Madame Fillietaz were away, only the family servants welcomed her. Wollstonecraft found herself alone in an immense residence in the ancient Marais district, north of the river Seine, quite near the centuries-old Temple that had once been the stronghold of the great militant order of the Christian Knights Templar.

Inside the square-towered Temple, the French royal family lived under close guard. More than a year earlier King Louis XVI had tried to join the stream of émigrés, aristocrats escaping France. With the assistance of the royal families of Europe and Britain and those sympathetic to the French crown, he had hoped to return to his country at the head of an army to put down the revolution. Instead, he and his family were captured and returned to Paris in humiliation. The king was now irremediably associated with the enemies of the revolution.

By 1792 Paris was not only hungry and angry, but in civil disarray. The revolution had dismantled piece by piece the institutions of the Old Regime: the government bureaus, the old parliament, the system of taxation, and the titles of hereditary nobles. Worse, the economic conditions, already perilous in the last stages of the Old Regime, were becoming desperate. With émigrés removing gold from the country, the paper currency rapidly decreased in value. French farmers were reluctant to sell their produce for increasingly worthless paper and instead hoarded their food. Parisians faced food scarcities and a steadily rising cost of living.

Meanwhile, feeling itself surrounded by hostile governments, France was at war with Hungary and Bohemia. In response to these wars declared as well as to wars threatened, nationalist fervor mounted all over the country, and the artisans, workers, mechanics, and shopkeepers of France were rallying to the revolution. Joining legions of recruits from the villages and rural hamlets of France, patriots from the southern port of Marseilles marched to Paris, singing the new anthem of their resistance to tyranny, "La Marseillaise." Betrayed by a king who had allied himself with their enemies, French peasants and workers from the countryside joined their compatriots in Paris. They placed their faith in the revolution to put food on their table and restore value to the money they earned.

On December 26 at nine o'clock in the morning, Mary Wollstonecraft was at her window at 22 rue Meslée when Louis XVI was led down the strangely quiet street to his trial. He moved along slowly, attended only by an occasional roll of the drum, a sound that made the quiet even more fearful. The streets were empty except for the National Guard, who clustered around his carriage. The silent Parisians looked out from behind closed windows, not one raising a cry or making an insulting gesture. The tribunal found the king guilty of crimes against the French people, and by a close vote the National Assembly ordered his execution.

On the morning of January 21, 1793, executioners held up the severed head of Louis XVI, formerly King of France, calling out "Long live the nation." Louis had ascended the scaffold calmly, and after bidding the drummers to fall silent, he said in a loud voice, "My people, I die an innocent man. I hope that my blood may secure the happiness of the French people."

Writing to Johnson, Wollstonecraft told him she wept when she saw Louis pass by, sitting in a simple coach "with more dignity than I expected from his character." Later, the house seemed achingly quiet. The servants' rooms were far away from her apartment, and no one else was at home. Not even a footstep interrupted the silence that seemed increasingly ghostly to her. Reluctant to put out the candle and go to sleep, she was sorry she had let out the cat. "I want to see something alive," she wrote to Johnson.

Death stalked Paris all that year. In August 1792, agitated by the new recruits who had come up from the south of France, the Parisian working class had overrun the Tuileries Palace, killing many of the Swiss Guard who had served the royal family. A month later a small number of rebellious soldiers declared they would not fight the enemies of France outside the borders while enemies inside were still free. In one onslaught, known afterward as "the September Massacres," the mob dragged 1,100 people from prisons. Some of them were enemies of the Revolution, but the majority were simple thieves, prostitutes, forgers, and vagrants, who were slaughtered on sight or given mock trials and immediate execution.

Paris was unsteady, reeling from waves of political hysteria and without the apparatus of civil authority to maintain order. But the glorious day "La Marseillaise" promised seemed to be dawning. Shortly before Wollstonecraft arrived, the Jacobins, as the French revolutionaries were called, organized a municipal government in Paris known as the commune. The Jacobins announced Year One of the French Republic, and proclaimed for the first time in France true universal male suffrage, the right of all French men to vote.

In the first weeks following the execution of Louis XVI in January 1793, Paris seemed quiet to Wollstonecraft, and she had begun to settle in. Although she was still embarrassed by her attempts to speak French, she was absorbed into a friendly international community of writers and thinkers who welcomed her as a celebrated author. Helen Maria Williams, a young English poet and novelist who lived in Paris, took her around to meet people. Her old acquaintance Thomas Paine lived nearby. Paine was now a French citizen and an elected deputy to the legislature, now called the National Convention. Wollstonecraft also renewed her friendship with an English acquaintance, Tom Christie, who was doing business in Paris, and with Joel Barlow, the American who had helped find a job for her brother Charles in the United States. The international group also included Swiss and Germans who were in Paris because of their republican sympathies. These were people well connected with the Gironde, the revolutionary French delegates in power. Through them Wollstonecraft met the political leader Jacques-Pierre Brissot de Warville, and came to admire Mme. Jeanne-Manon Roland, a Girondist and politician whose home was the meeting place for discussions about democracy.

There were other reasons to admire the Girondists beyond their support of the rights of men. These people were also friends of woman's rights. The Marquis de Condorcet, architect of the first French constitution, had argued for the rights of women, and in its early stages the revolution was sympathetic to

The government in London was fearful that the revolution in France might prove contagious, and it launched a propaganda war to heap abuse upon the new French republic. Blaming mob violence on democracy, this cartoon claims that "equality" leads to misery and madness.

THE CONTRAST
1792

BRITISH LIBERTY

FRENCH LIBERTY

RELIGION.   MORALITY.
LOYALTY OBEDIENCE TO THE LAWS
INDEPENDANCE PERSONAL SECURITY
JUSTICE INHERITANCE PROTECTION
PROPERTY. INDUSTRY NATIONAL PROSPERITY
HAPPINESS

ATHEISM   PERJURY.
REBELLION TREASON ANARCHY MURDER
EQUALITY MADNESS CRUELTY INJUSTICE
TREACHERY INGRATITUDE IDLENESS
FAMINE NATIONAL & PRIVATE RUIN.
MISERY

WHICH IS BEST

women's property rights. These revolutionaries were willing to question the divine right of fathers, brothers, and husbands, as well as kings. In September 1792 delegates to the National Convention passed new, liberal divorce laws. Deputies even suggested appointing women to the civil service and educating them for business, professions, and teaching.

Even more shocking to many, radical members of Parisian women's clubs patrolled the streets in red-and-white trousers. Their men's clothing and aggressive behavior led some people sympathetic to women's rights to worry that women were casting aside traditional notions of proper female deportment. One of the most outrageous women was Olympe de Gouges, whose mother was a butcher. Thumbing her nose at custom, de Gouges challenged men to duels and asked Maximilien Robespierre, leader of the National Convention, to swim with her in the Seine. She wrote plays, argued for a national women's theater, and printed her own revolutionary pamphlets.

With so many people in France interested in women's rights, Mary Wollstonecraft was treated as an important person joining a vital and ongoing debate. She wrote in February to Ruth Barlow, Joel's wife, that she was "almost overwhelmed with civility." Even though the inevitable war between monarchical England and revolutionary France broke out that month, she chose to remain where she was. An acquaintance offered her a place in a coach leaving for the channel crossing, but she declined the offer. She had expected to be away from London for only six weeks and had not made arrangements to vacate the Store Street lodgings. But now, for better or worse, she cast her lot with France.

Once again Wollstonecraft was writing. Joseph Johnson was urging her to write down her observations of the Revolution. Since she owed him money for her passage, she set about her task at once, writing informal observations in the form of letters home. Some months later, she penned her more considered observations of the French Revolution, which Johnson later published in London. Unlike many of the people at home, who were now in the grips of a strong anti-French fervor, she had not lost confidence in the Revolution after the September Massacres. People could not suddenly behave rationally, she argued, when their govern-ments had kept them children for so long. And children, she wrote, "will do mischief when they meddle with sharp edged tools." The Revolution was just such a sharp instrument.

Still, to the alarm of Wollstonecraft, the sharp tool of the Revolution was raised against friends of the rights of man. In the spring of 1793 Robespierre had gained control of the National Convention and set up a system of revolutionary courts. Such courts were improvements on the quick "justice" that had been meted out at the time of the September Massacres. With these courts in place, however, Robespierre attacked the more moderate Girondists, who were reluctant to create the strong centralized government he was building in Paris. The Girondists, many of them from outside Paris, were afraid that the Parisian radicals were creating a dictatorship. Nor were the Girondists willing to institute the economic reforms that Robespierre's faction, the Jacobins, argued were critical to feed Paris. Even as many people in Paris were becoming rich, the cost of food kept most people hungry.

As she witnessed the political convulsions, Wollstonecraft was startled by the financial scheming going on around her. She had always been hostile to projects that aimed only at making money. Now, she observed, the aristocracy of birth was being "levelled to the ground only to make room for that of riches." She loathed "the principle of commerce" that seemed to be widespread.

Among her new friends in Paris was an American adventurer named Gilbert Imlay. He was a man in whom the principle of commerce had taken profound root. Imlay was tall, slim, and well-spoken, the kind of American whom Europeans found charming. He told everyone that he had grown up in Kentucky and indeed had recently published his first book about the American Western territories. To Parisians, he carried about him the whiff of sagebrush, the scent and romance of the frontier. Wollstonecraft loved the "simplicity" of his character. In a letter she wrote to Everina about Imlay, she said, "Having been brought up in the interior parts of America, he is a most natural, unaffected creature."

But there was nothing simple about Imlay. He was less than completely candid about his past. He had grown up in New Jersey, not Kentucky. Although he called himself "captain," he had not risen above the rank of lieutenant in the American army. After serving in the American Revolution he had gone to Kentucky, hungry for land and for the money that speculation in land might bring him. In the course of a few short years there, he had bought and sold thousands of acres, but the profits slipped away from him. Only debts followed him to France.

He came to Paris, as had so many others, to make his fortune, as well as to applaud the Revolution. Although Wollstonecraft was hostile to money making, the spirit of democracy in the young Republic welcomed the enterprise of self-made men. Schemes for making fortunes abounded, and Imlay was a part of the excitement. In Paris he hoped to interest the Girondist leader Brissot in a land scheme in the

Mississippi Valley. Brissot was interested, but, like so many of Imlay's plans, the business venture did not succeed.

Wollstonecraft met Imlay at the home of Thomas Christie in the spring of 1793. At first she did not think much of him, although she intrigued him. She was, after all, the celebrated Mary Wollstonecraft, animated, attractive, and trailing a reputation of writing an argument on women's rights. Imlay managed to sit near her and to talk with her. Conversation was easy. He sensed his business dealings did not please her, and he was cautious about mentioning them. But their political and social sympathies were alike. They both opposed a state religion and believed in progress and perfectibility. Imlay arrived in France with credentials as an abolitionist, a spokesperson against the practice of slavery still flourishing in the United States. He was a defender of the newly ratified American Constitution, with its carefully framed balance of power and its transfer of power from the states to a strengthened central government.

Wollstonecraft also found Imlay appealing as a romantic figure. Later, in her novel *Maria* she described him as "tall, handsome, lean, natural, warm-hearted, cheerful, manly." Imlay knew how to talk sweetly. As their friendship grew, he sketched for her the prospect of returning together to the United States to live on a farm far from the corruption and tumult of Europe. Wollstonecraft's mother had been fed the same dream by her husband, Edward. Mary Wollstonecraft was ready for such a suitor. The attraction to Fuseli had ended in humiliating rejection. Imlay won her heart. Joel Barlow, writing to his wife in the spring of 1793, gossiped happily about her, "Between you and me—I believe she has a sweetheart."

Their romance flourished throughout that spring just as her position as an English subject was becoming dangerous. By day Paris was seized in almost febrile jubilation. There were revolutionary parades and ceremonial burnings of the fleur-de-lis, the three-petaled white iris flower emblem of the monarchy that now was loathed and reviled. By night the police roamed the streets and searched houses from attic to cellar for enemies of the Revolution. Long lines formed in the evening outside shops, the people hoping to buy scant supplies of sugar, soap, and candles when the shopkeepers open for business in the morning., Foreigners were watched carefully, and by law heads of households had to inscribe the names of residents on their doorposts. When Robespierre proposed the expulsion of all foreigners from France in September 1793, Imlay registered Wollstonecraft at the American embassy as his wife. The Jacobins worried less about Americans, since the United States, unlike Britain, was a republic and was not at war with revolutionary France. "Mrs. Imlay" was a safer name than "Miss Wollstonecraft."

Still, they did not legally marry. Both partners despised marriage as a formal contract that did not touch the heart. Wollstonecraft believed she had made a "sacred" bond and archly told her friends she would not swear obedience to her lover, as the traditional marriage ceremony would have required.

Meanwhile, the Girondists and their friends fell under grave suspicion when Robespierre consolidated his power. The international community gathered for furtive conversation, and some made plans to leave France hastily. To avoid suspicion as an enemy of the Revolution, Helen Maria Williams burned her manuscripts and the papers Mme. Roland had entrusted to her. Thomas Christie was denounced and imprisoned. Later, he was released, and fled to Switzerland. The arrests and executions of some of the fine people she had met in Paris repelled and appalled Wollstonecraft. Even Thomas Paine, who had fled England ahead of arrest, was now at risk in Paris. "Down fell the temple of despotism," Wollstonecraft wrote about the Bastille, "but despotism had not been buried in its ruins." She could not ignore the grave risk she posed to the Fillietaz family. With Imlay's help she moved to Neuilly, then a small country village northwest of Paris. There, in early summer 1793, she found a cottage set in a garden overlooking a field and woods. This was not the American farm Imlay had promised, but in Neuilly she spent some brief and happy months.

Wollstonecraft took her books with her from Paris and settled in to write about the Revolution, as Johnson had suggested. Hoping for a better future, she wrote happily to Eliza, promising her "brighter days are in store for you." The United States that Imlay was picturing would have employment for her sisters as well. Imlay visited Wollstonecraft regularly. Because she often met him at the tollgate in the Paris city wall, *la barrière*, he called her his "barrier girl."

Life was often sweet at Neuilly. The old gardener who lived nearby brought Mary grapes that he dotingly allowed her alone to eat. He hovered protectively and warned her about brigands in the nearby forests at night. Laughing at his fears, Wollstonecraft roamed the countryside on her own and one day walked as far as Versailles. She found the deserted royal palace and strolled through the empty corridors, finding them eerie in their silence. Later, she described for Johnson the sad gloom that seemed to haunt the place.

Her old melancholy was never very far away, even in Neuilly. Sadly for her, Imlay went to the port city of Le Havre often to attend to business. With an English blockade preventing cargoes from reaching France at Le Havre, there was money to be made for those who could move shipments through. An unhappy pattern formed. Imlay would leave on business and Wollstonecraft, worried that he did not love her, would become depressed and quarrelsome. "Of late we are always separating," she wrote to him, "crack!—crack!—and away you go." In another letter she wrote, "I hate commerce," and did not love his "money-getting face either."

Imlay sometimes wrote that he was trying to make money so that they might have a happy life together. To one of these letters, Wollstonecraft responded, "If you make any of your plans answer—it is well, I do not think a little money inconvenient; but, should they fail, we will struggle cheerfully together—drawn closer by the pinching blasts of poverty." She knew that her disdain for his work and her self-pity alarmed him, but when her melancholy claimed her, she could not silence her anxiety. "Cherish me with that dignified tenderness, which I have found only in you," she wrote to Imlay, "and your own dear girl will try to keep under a quickness of feeling, that has sometimes given you pain." "I am afraid I have vexed you," she wrote another time, "there is nothing I would not suffer to make you happy."

Imlay could be reassuring. While Wollstonecraft was keeping house in Neuilly and he was in Paris or Le Havre, he described charming pictures of the home they would make together, scenes upon which she happily enlarged. She put aside some of her books for them to read together and imagined Imlay reading aloud while she mended her stockings. She imagined her head on his shoulder, her eyes fixed on the "little creatures," their future children, that would be clinging about his knees. "I did not absolutely determine that there should be six—if you have not set your heart on this round number."

There were good reasons to tease Imlay about fatherhood. In November, Wollstonecraft felt some "gentle twitches" and realized she was pregnant. Suddenly the responsibility of another life weighed upon her. She worried that the anxieties to which she was so often susceptible might harm her unborn child. One day, hurt from lifting a heavy log, she sat down "in an agony," until she felt the twitches again. The next day she wrote to Imlay, tell me "over and over again, that your happiness (and you deserve to be happy!) is closely connected with mine."

When she felt confident and lighthearted, she could be blithe in her reproaches. Come home soon, she warned, or "I will throw your slippers out the window and be off—nobody knows where." Or she could be witty and amusing. "Amongst the feathered race," she complained, "whilst the hen keeps the young warm, her mate stays by to cheer her, but it is sufficient for man to condescend to get a child, in order to claim it. A man is a tyrant." But more frequently her temper rose. He was so much more cheerful than she, so less concerned by their separations. How could she believe his reassurances that he loved her? When she was hurt, she withdrew and became cold, just as she had years before when she believed Jane Arden or Fanny Blood was indifferent to her.

While she was in Neuilly, Robespierre's Reign of Terror continued. One day when she went to Paris, she walked to

the Place de la Revolution, where the guillotine stood across from the Tuileries garden. To her horror, there was fresh blood on the street. She could not keep from exclaiming out loud, although worried passersby quieted her and told her that her indignation was dangerous. In November Mme. Roland was guillotined. Brave and upright, Jeanne-Manon Roland mounted the block, calling out to the goddess of liberty and asking how many had died in her name. Helen Maria Williams, the young English writer, was rousted out of her bed and put in prison. When Wollstonecraft was told that Brissot and 20 deputies of the Gironde government had been guillotined in one group, she fainted. It seemed to her that she had never known such horror before.

In Paris, 2,639 people died during the Terror, only 8 percent of them aristocrats. By modern standards, after two destructive world wars, the number of deaths is modest. Still, the clatter of the two-wheeled tumbrels taking the condemned to execution; the warning clang of the tocsin, which were the bells announcing the tumbrels' approach; and the snap of the great ax of the guillotine—these were not the music of a rational

The gallant Madame Manon Roland was brought to the guillotine by Robespierre during the Reign of Terror. Wollstonecraft had admired Madame Roland and wrote from France to a friend in England, "My God, how many victims fall beneath the sword and the Guillotine! My blood runs cold, and I sicken at the thoughts of a Revolution which costs so much blood and bitter tears."

VISITING VERSAILLES DURING THE FRENCH REVOLUTION

Mary Wollstonecraft visited the palace at Versailles while she was living near Paris in 1793. Several years earlier the French king and queen had been forced by the French mob to abandon Versailles for Paris, where they were held as prisoners of the Revolution. Struck by the bleakness of a once-glorious palace, Wollstonecraft was consoled that a more moral and just society would replace Versailles.

How silent is now Versailles!—The solitary foot, that mounts the sumptuous stair-case, rests on each landing-place, whilst the eye traverses the void, almost expecting to see the strong images of fancy burst into life.—The train of the Louises, like the posterity of the Banquoes, pass in solemn sadness, pointing at the nothingness of grandeur, fading away on the cold canvas, which covers the nakedness of the spacious walls—whilst the gloominess of the atmosphere gives a deeper shade to the gigantic figures, that seem to be sinking into the embraces of death.

Warily entering the endless apartments, half shut up, the fleeting shadow of the pensive wanderer, reflected in long glasses, that vainly gleam in every direction, slacken the nerves, without appalling the heart; though lacivious pictures, in which grace varnishes voluptuousness, no longer seductive, strike continually home to the bosom the melancholy moral, that anticipates the frozen lesson of experience. The very air is chill, seeming to clog the breath; and the wasting dampness of destruction appears to be stealing into the vast pile, on every side . . .

Lo! this was the palace of the great king!—the abode of magnificence!—Who has broken the charm?—Why does it now inspire only pity?—Why;—because nature, smiling around, presents to the imagination materials to build farms, and hospitable mansions, where, without raising idle admiration, that gladness will reign, which opens the heart to benevolence, and that industry, which renders innocent pleasure sweet.

society improving itself. Wollstonecraft did not believe that Paris in 1793 met the standard of reason she had esteemed since her earlier days in the pews at Newington Green. This fear and bloodshed were not what she and her friends celebrated around Johnson's dinner table. "The ferocity of the partisans [had produced]," she wrote, "dreadful effects. . . . The mobs were barbarous beyond the tiger's cruelty." Yet this deplorable violence had broken out, she believed, because the monarchy and aristocracy had corrupted the nation for so long. She still believed that progress would be served in France. Just as a good body throws off illness, the nation would cure itself finally. But her confidence in the innate goodness of the human soul was badly shaken. To Johnson she wrote, "I am not become an atheist, I assure you . . . yet I begin to fear that vice, or if you will, evil is the grand mobile of action."

With the fall of the Girondists, hopes for equality for women in France also vanished. Under Robespierre, deputies of the Convention argued that women were naturally inferior to men. In July 1793, when Charlotte Corday, hoping to rouse sympathy for the Girondists, murdered the journalist Jean-Paul Marat, she was depicted as a madwoman, an emblem of a woman diseased by arguments for women's rights. Gone were the prospects for equal education for women and for full political rights. French women, so many of whom marched bravely for the Revolution, had to wait until 1945 for the right to vote.

Early in the new year 1794, Wollstonecraft felt physically unwell, prey to stomach disorders and anxious that her melancholy moods were hurting her unborn baby. She resolved to exercise and so walked about in Neuilly, no matter what the weather. As childbirth approached, she was calmer. She joined Imlay in Le Havre and, for a while, kept house for him happily, ordering his linen shirts, arranging lamb roasts for dinner in front of a wood fire, and keeping up the healthful exercise of daily walks. Meanwhile, she finished her essay on the French Revolution for Johnson, determined to conclude the writing

Fanny Imlay, whose birth to Gilbert Imlay and Mary Wollstonecraft was recorded in Le Havre, France, was a "wonderfully intelligent" baby according to her mother. To Imlay, who was often absent, Wollstonecraft wrote, "My little darling is a sweet child. She is all vivacity or softness . . . I cannot, I find, long be angry with you, whilst I am kissing her for resembling you."

before her baby was born. In May 1794 Fanny Imlay was born. She was named for Fanny Blood, Mary's childhood friend.

The birth was easy. The French nurse who attended Wollstonecraft told her she should "make children for the Republic." Wollstonecraft was contemptuous of traditional polite attitudes toward childbirth that treated new mothers like invalids. Instead of spending the customary month resting indoors, or "lying in," she walked about the day after Fanny was born and a week later was outside. Instead of swaddling Fanny in wraps, she kept her baby in loose, airy clothing and gave her plenty of fresh air.

Motherhood came easily to Wollstonecraft. She teased her friend Ruth Barlow that she had knitted the caps too small for Fanny, underestimating the "quantity of brains she was to have." Imlay joked that little Fanny nursed with such vigor and spirit, she would probably one day write the second volume of the *Rights of Woman*. Wollstonecraft was proud of nursing Fanny. Most middle-class women sent their babies to be breast-fed by other mothers in the neighborhood, a practice called wet nursing. Wollstonecraft, however, believed that breast-feeding secured the bond between mother and infant. Fanny was, Wollstonecraft believed, an "uncommonly healthy baby," which she attributed to her own "good" and "natural" manner of nursing the infant.

Fanny Imlay's earliest days passed peacefully, except for a frightening attack of smallpox. Wollstonecraft wrote proudly to Everina that she followed her own sound sense in nursing

Fanny through the illness and disregarded medical advice by bathing the baby in warm water twice daily. Fanny was well again, but Imlay was restless and making plans to leave. In September he left Le Havre for London to oversee the export of scarce goods—building materials, grain, and ammunition—into France. Wollstonecraft took Fanny and returned to Paris, which was safer now because earlier that summer Robespierre's government had fallen. As Wollstonecraft and Imlay separated, Imlay promised to return to Paris in two months, a promise he did not keep.

The journey from Le Havre to Paris with Fanny was a nightmare. The carriage overturned four times and, once mother and daughter arrived in Paris, Wollstonecraft discovered that the maid she had hired to help with Fanny was pregnant and unable to do much work. Fanny was a spirited and vivacious baby whose growth Wollstonecraft loved to chronicle. "Besides looking at me," she wrote to Imlay about their daughter, "there are three other things which delight her—to ride in a coach, to look at a scarlet waistcoat, and hear loud music." But Wollstonecraft needed help in looking after her if she was going to continue writing.

Meanwhile, the provisional government that followed Robespierre's had restored freedom of the press. Wollstonecraft hoped that at last social improvements would follow as intellectuals in Paris felt that a siege was lifted. Arrangements at home also improved when Wollstonecraft recruited a new maid, Marguerite, and added another nursemaid to her household. With two helpers, she felt she would be able to be a good mother without becoming a "slave" to her child. She planned to practice her French and to be out in the world. She teased Imlay she might fall in love with one or two admirers if he did not hurry back. But the tall, good-looking American was the only man she wanted, and she remained loyal to him.

It was revitalizing to be again among the international community in Paris. One visitor, Archibald Hamilton Rowan, who had fled political reprisals in Dublin for his republican politics, came across Wollstonecraft one day at a street festival. He saw an English-speaking lady followed by her maid with an infant in her arms. "Her manners were interesting and her conversation spirited," noted Rowan later. Someone whispered to him that the woman was the author of *A Vindication of the Rights of Woman.* "This is Miss Wollstonecraft, parading about with a child at her heels," Rowan responded. He recorded the scene in a letter to his wife, adding that he befriended Wollstonecraft. Any time he stopped by to visit her, he was confident of a "dish of tea" and "an hour's rational conversation."

Wollstonecraft's natural vivacity rose in Paris, as well as the strength of her convictions that relationships must be based only on love. As Rowan and Wollstonecraft drank tea together, he heard her argue that "no motive on earth ought to make a man and wife live together a moment after mutual love and regard are gone." Now that she had known romantic love with Gilbert Imlay, she was retreating from the argument in *Vindication* that it is better when husband and wife are only friends. As time passed, though, she confronted the painful possibility that the love she shared with Imlay was perhaps no longer returned.

Imlay's absence stretched on, and the times of his promised returns arrived and passed again and again, Wollstonecraft found it harder to believe his protests that business affairs were keeping him away. At last she suggested to him that other reasons might be preventing his return. "If a wandering of the heart, or even a caprice of the imagination detains you—there is an end to all my hopes of happiness."

Such thinking was calamitous because Wollstonecraft responded to emotional distress with physical decline. Moreover, the winter of 1794–95 was particularly bitter. In France, rivers and canals froze. Food scarcities were widespread, and people were hungry. Wood and coal were almost unobtainable. By January 1795 Wollstonecraft was ill, and her money was dwindling. Expecting Imlay all these months, she had not taken the necessary steps to live independently. Merely to find wood and coal, she should have hired a servant to search all day. Unable to shake her illness, she worried that a weakness might enter her lungs and develop into tuberculosis. It seemed to her she must think about a caretaker for Fanny if she should die.

Imlay's letters were not frequent or lengthy, although he protested that some of them must have gone astray. In no letter did he ever claim he wanted to be free of her. Again and again he protested he was only working to acquire money for their life together. If Mary protested she would be happy to be poor, he confessed he needed some "secondary comforts." But he promised, "Our being together is paramount to every other consideration." When he put off his return to Paris indefinitely, Wollstonecraft poured out her misery to him. At last he proposed that she join him in London. She responded that England had lost all charms for her. She felt repugnance for her own country—almost horror, in fact. She was convinced that Fanny would grow up to be miserable in England. A child without married parents would face ostracism or reproof in more conservative England. France was freer.

Wollstonecraft meant to stay in Paris. On the advice of her doctors, she weaned Fanny to restore her own health. Additionally, she had one or two plans for earning her keep. But Imlay wrote, "Come to any port and I will fly down to my two dear girls with a heart all their own." Finally, she believed him.

In April 1795 Wollstonecraft returned to Le Havre to pick up linens from her house there and set out for England. The trip was ill-fated from the beginning. The pilot was clumsy, and the ship ran aground in the harbor at Le Havre. The passengers were forced to disembark. Wollstonecraft returned to the house she had shared so briefly with Imlay to wait for the next sailing. She wrote to Rowan that she "seemed to be counting the ticking of a clock and there is no clock here." At last, a few days later, the ship sailed. She, Fanny, and the nursemaid Marguerite arrived in Brighton. With favorable winds, the journey would have only been five hours. Mary Wollstonecraft was home again. "Here we are my love—" she wrote to Imlay, who was not there to meet her.

THE SOLITARY
TRAVELER

*Wollstonecraft repre-
sented in the style of
French revolutionary
women. The poet
Robert Southey, writing
about her at this time,
said, "her eyes are light
brown, and though the
lid of them is affected by
a little paralysis, they
are the most meaning I
ever saw."*

Mary Wollstonecraft had been gone for almost two and a half years. She was returning to England with a child to search for an indifferent lover. Now she had seen the Revolution at work in France, and, while she still hoped that societies could perfect themselves by exercising reason, she was less hopeful now that the process would be easy. Wollstonecraft came to London reluctantly. Her friends at home would be worried for her now that she was the mother of a child whose father was so unreliable. Then too her sisters, to whom she had described Gilbert Imlay so favorably, might understandably come to London expecting hospitality and assistance. How would the less-appealing truth about Imlay escape their careful notice?

Nor was it pleasant to be back in England, where feelings against the Revolution in France ran so high. William Pitt's government convinced the British that France was enslaved by madmen, idolatrous, bloodthirsty zealots who raised the standard of the rights of man as a call to mayhem, havoc, and misery. Anti-Jacobin societies had spread throughout England. A year earlier Pitt's government had put the leaders of the London Corresponding Society, a political reform group, on trial for treason.

In fact, this sober group of shopkeepers, craftsmen, and apprentices was not as revolutionary as Pitt charged. Their program for reform was simple and often phrased in the language of ancient English rights. Loyal to their monarch, King George III, they asked for annual parliaments, wider voting rights, and abandonment of such parliamentary dinosaurs as "pocket boroughs," which permitted privileged aristocrats to handpick a member of Parliament.

Treason was no small charge. The punishment for high treason was still to be hanged, drawn, and quartered: After being hanged the still-living, unfortunate victim would be cut down, disemboweled, and then hacked to death. Death by guillotine was, by comparison, an act of exquisite mercy. So dreadful was this manner of execution that it was seldom enacted. Nor was it in this instance since the leaders of the London Corresponding Society were found innocent and released.

To be sure, the times were not quiet in England. In the summer and winter months of 1795, there were food short-

Public discontent was high in the 1790s when crops failed and food was scarce and expensive. When an assassin fired on George III, breaking the glass of his carriage, the government claimed republican sympathizers were to blame.

The REPUBLICAN - ATTACK.

ages and popular discontent. Rioters and agitators sold inflammatory pamphlets with titles like *Happy Reign of George the Last*. On one memorable autumn day, a large, noisy crowd of Londoners hissed and booed the king as he rode in his carriage to open Parliament. While men yelled "Down with George" and "Bread!" suddenly someone threw a stone and broke a window of the king's carriage. George III was safe, but no one could ignore the awesome parallels of such riots with the revolution in France. Only two years earlier King Louis XVI had been ceremoniously conducted to the execution block and beheaded. Could the English monarchy be traveling in the same direction as the French republic?

Pitt struck back again and again. Claiming a member of the London Corresponding Society had thrown the stone at the king, Pitt stirred up fears that a network of British clubs, like those of the French, might be planning a revolution in England. Later in the year he passed anti-sedition acts. These banned political meetings of more than 50 persons, and made speaking or writing against the king a treasonable act. He suspended the writ of habeas corpus (literally meaning "hold the body"), which for centuries had guaranteed that no one could be imprisoned in England without being formally charged with a crime. Ancient British freedoms—to speak and write one's mind, and to know the legal charge against one—were trampled underfoot. Small wonder that Wollstonecraft believed the English had lost all common sense.

Moreover, it seemed to her that Gilbert Imlay had lost his reason as well. When she met him on arriving in London, he took her to furnished rooms, but his manner was cool and remote. Longing for reassurance that he meant to love her and live with her, Wollstonecraft found it difficult to find anything in London familiar and welcoming. The Christies had moved back to London, and Rachel Christie in particular was her friend. But it was agonizing for Wollstonecraft to have to write to her sisters and pretend that she could not have them visit when she had always opened her home to them.

Explaining this to Eliza, she wrote, "When Mr. Imlay and I united our fate together he was without fortune." She would do what she could for Eliza, she said, but she asked her not to visit. "The presence of a third person interrupts or destroys domestic happiness," she apologized. Eliza was outraged. "Good God what a letter!" she fumed to Everina. "When did I wish to live with her? at what time wish for a moment to interrupt their domestic happiness?" Eliza sent an angry letter back, addressed: "To the author of the 'Rights of Woman.'" Eliza and Mary Wollstonecraft never healed the breach.

Worse, far worse, Wollstonecraft could no longer pretend that Imlay was faithful to her. As she had feared, Imlay had found another mistress, an actress from a strolling theater company. Wollstonecraft flung angry, brave, and defiant words at him, but unhappiness overwhelmed her. She took an overdose of laudanum, a common tranquilizer at that time, and had to be revived by an anxious Rachel Christie. Her friends urged her to rally, to think of her child, to carry on. Imlay, too, was shaken. The unnatural death of such a famous woman because of unrequited love for him would present him to the world in an unflattering light. It was easy for him to be reassuring once again and easy for Wollstonecraft to be deceived. Perhaps some domestic arrangement could be worked out, she hoped. Perhaps they simply needed time to think.

Meanwhile, Gilbert Imlay had an astounding proposition to offer. He had business in Scandinavia that needed supervision and asked Wollstonecraft to travel there on his behalf. The proposal was attractive to both of them. Wollstonecraft would leave London, and, for some time at least, they could avoid a crisis. She accepted his proposal and made plans to travel to Sweden, where she would meet business associates of Imlay.

In June, only a few months after she arrived in England, Wollstonecraft set sail with Fanny and Marguerite. They made an odd traveling group, since Scandinavian countries attracted few tourists. Most visitors to Sweden, Norway, and Denmark were traders. Certainly few of them were women alone with infants.

Imlay gave Wollstonecraft papers describing her as his "best friend and wife," who was attending to one of his business ventures that had gone awry. A small fortune that he had invested in the venture was at risk. Some time before, Imlay had purchased a ship, which he registered in Norway. He had loaded it with expensive cargo, bars of silver and silver plate ware, which he was hoping to move through the British blockade and into France. To his dismay, the captain he hired had taken the ship to Denmark, and now Danish courts were going to decide who actually owned the ship. Wollstonecraft found herself in the unlikely role of Imlay's agent, representing the business interests she frankly despised. Still, Wollstonecraft had always found traveling exciting; and activity was revitalizing, whereas sitting in London brooding was dangerously debilitating.

With the baby and her nursemaid, Wollstonecraft traveled first to the port city of Hull in northern England. From there she would take a ship to the Swedish coastal town of Gothenburg. Unfortunately, the weather in Hull was not favorable for sailing. Several times the captain alerted her to hurry on board and prepare to sail, only to find that the wind had changed. And Marguerite grew seasick from the listing of the boat even while it was standing anchored to shore.

With time to pass waiting for better weather, Wollstonecraft boarded with a physician's family in town. One day, her hosts agreed to an interesting diversion. They took a carriage to Wollstonecraft's old childhood home of Beverley, which was quite near to Hull. At first she ran eagerly over her old familiar walks, but on reflection the town seemed less pleasant to her. Beverley seemed to have shrunk, and the lives of her old neighbors struck her as narrow. Many of them lived in the same houses they had always occupied, while she had gone to London, visited Lisbon, lived in Paris, and was now traveling to the remote and rugged landscapes of northern Europe. When conversations turned to politics, she was startled by the hostility of her old neighbors to the French Revolution. Beverley seemed to have become more aristocrat-

ic in its sympathies, while she, and everyone she admired, believed that the age of aristocrats was ending.

It was not difficult to turn her back on Beverley and begin her journey. At last the winds were favorable, and Wollstonecraft, with her daughter and nursemaid, set off for Gothenburg. She was a good sailor and had borne the trip to Lisbon with no seasickness. However, she had never traveled with a child and nurse. This trip was nightmarish. They were 11 days crossing the North Sea on a cargo ship ill-fitted for passengers. Fanny was teething and uncomfortable, Marguerite was seasick. When they reached the coast of Sweden, again without a good wind, the captain mistook his bearings and sailed beyond Gothenburg Bay. They were forced to wait hours in calm waters for the lighthouse pilot to send out a boat to bring the small party to shore. A lighthouse pilot was an important person on the coastline. He was responsible for guarding any unfortunate ships wrecked on the coastal rocks so that their cargo would not be stolen and their sailors not left to drown by villagers turned bandits and murderers. But the pilot was slow to appear. Finally, Wollstonecraft paid the reluctant captain to violate company rules and send out one of his own boats. "Men with common

Merchant ships made their way into Stockholm's harbor, past cannons defending the city. The cities, coasts, and country of Scandinavia were unfamiliar to the English, so Mary Wollstonecraft's poetic descriptions of her travels there sold well and were critically acclaimed.

minds seldom break through general rules," Wollstonecraft observed caustically.

Sailors rowed the two women and the baby to shore, searching the coastline for some welcoming people. All the while Marguerite moaned of the dangers their little party might face in such a desolate land. At last they found the lighthouse pilot, a man of some education who spoke English. Now he found himself, surprisingly, the host of such an unusal traveling party of a mother, her child, and a nursemaid.

Happily, the pilot's home was clean and welcoming. The floor was strewn with fragrant sprigs of juniper that kept the house pleasant smelling and cleaner underfoot, and the bedding was a sparkling-white coarse muslin. Though the pilot's wife spoke no English, she could appraise the status of her guests. Noticing that Wollstonecraft had the uncalloused hands of a lady, she set out all the food she possessed on white linen. Wollstonecraft enjoyed the simple meal of fish, butter, milk, and cheese after the unappetizing provisions the cargo ship offered during the days at sea.

Now her land journey began. She was on the road for four months, sometimes a solitary woman while Fanny and Marguerite waited for her in rented lodgings. She traveled among men with whom she shared no common language. Tracking down Imlay's lost cargo, she had to negotiate arrangements for ferries, send servants ahead of her for fresh horses, bargain with innkeepers in desolate country for rough beds and, at times, cold food.

Early on, however, Wollstonecraft found another and more congenial purpose for her voyage. Wherever her gaze fell, there was an impressive landscape to describe. Whatever company she was in, there was an interesting society to document. Just as she had observed the Revolution while living in Paris, here she became an observer of Scandinavia, describing all she had seen and done that day. The Northlands in summertime provided her with generous light, so that she needed no candle even late at night.

In Gothenburg Bay, the pilot found an English-speaking family nearby and, promising her good company, he took Wollstonecraft to meet them. Her host had a reputation for humor and a family of vivacious and friendly daughters who amused Fanny. At dinner Wollstonecraft played her part as travel writer and turned to her host for information about Sweden. He replied bluntly that she was "a woman of observation" because she asked him "men's questions."

Wollstonecraft asked such questions of the people she met all over Scandinavia, as she observed and evaluated the justice systems, the economies, and the class relations of the lands through which she traveled. These were not, she believed, well-educated countries. Even among the fortunate few who were educated, she did not find the knowledge of science and the fascination with scientific experimentation that was common among the intellectuals she had admired in Newington Green and London. Some practices she found unsanitary and unpleasant, such as over-dressing children, over-salting food, drinking brandy with meals, and choking visitors with clouds of tobacco smoke. Even wellborn ladies in Sweden did not seem particularly clean, and she noticed they took little exercise.

The lives of peasant women were more pitiful. "The men stand up for the dignity of men by oppressing the women," she complained. These women were left to do the most menial work, she learned. In winter they scrubbed their linen in freezing rivers until their hands were cracked and bleeding. Meanwhile, even men standing nearby would not "disgrace their manhood by carrying a tub to lighten their burden". Imagining Imlay responding to her, she wrote to him, "Still harping on the same subject, you will exclaim. How can I avoid it, when most of the struggles of an eventful life have been occasioned by the oppressed state of my sex." There were, however, worse things to learn.

One day in Denmark, traveling back into town from a business appointment, Wollstonecraft came upon a crowd beginning to leave a public execution. Opposed to capital punishment in all forms, Wollstonecraft was horrified to see that well-dressed women had brought children to watch the condemned man die. Later, she was told that persons suffering from the effects of strokes drank the criminal's blood as a cure. When she protested that this was a "horrible violation of nature," a Danish woman asked how Wollstonecraft could know that it was not a cure. Wollstonecraft dropped the argument; against ignorance so dense, she felt debate was useless. As she had argued in *A Vindication of the Rights of Woman,* not much could be expected from people until education was widespread.

Although she regretted the ignorance she found, Wollstonecraft applauded the sympathy for France and its revolution that ran high wherever she traveled. In Norway she found her hosts defending Robespierre as a crusader for freedom, leaving her to argue he had monstrously executed lovers of France and lovers of liberty. To her delight, her hosts happily sang republican songs in translation and cheered French victories against their enemies. When she remembered the political repression in England and the smug defense of aristocracy in Beverley, Wollstonecraft was pleased to be among sympathizers of the rights of man. Ignorance may still have claimed a vast reach of Scandinavian society, but her hosts were raising the lamp of the Enlightenment.

Even more restorative to her goodwill and good health was the natural wilderness of Scandinavia, which stimulated and refreshed her. From her first night in Gothenburg Bay, as the great craggy coastline darkened, she chronicled her feelings as she saw them reflected on seascape, woodland, and pasture. The dark rocks beating back the tide seemed sheltering. Nearby on small patches of land covered with wildflowers, goats and a few straggling cows grazed peacefully. She felt the horrors of bloodshed in France recede, as well as the anguish that had more recently driven her to take laudanum. Earlier that day Fanny, now over a year old, delighted to be able to ramble after the sea voyage, found strawberries; and Wollstonecraft found wild pansies growing between rocks.

She took them as a good omen and pressed one in a book. Heartsease, she remembered, was the folk name for the flower. She felt suddenly and unexpectedly happy.

Mary Wollstonecraft was of course always an object of great curiosity, whether she was traveling alone, carrying Fanny, or with the nursemaid trailing after her. She knew people found her solitariness dreadful and interesting. Even her clothing, from London and Paris, excited attention. It was as if she had "dropped from the clouds in a strange land."

Then too there was something arresting in her appearance. Wollstonecraft felt that her weariness gave her a look of "peculiar delicacy." When she parted from Fanny and Marguerite for some weeks to travel alone in Norway, she was melancholy. She missed her baby daughter and thought about the people she had loved who had gone from her life: Fanny Blood, Gilbert Imlay. One day she watched a child walking by the side of the road with her father. She imagined the child's mother at home, preparing dinner. Her own loneliness never felt so painful. She had no love of cooking, she admitted to herself, but she envied the family in that simple cottage. As for her own household, she remembered that she was returning to her baby, who would probably never know a father's love.

She and Imlay were still writing unhappy letters to each other. "We must meet shortly or part forever," Wollstonecraft warned. He wrote that they were too dissimilar, their minds not congenial. Still, he would try to "cherish tenderness" toward her. Mary replied angrily that he need not injure himself with such exertions. With painful self-awareness, she realized she exhausted him. She would try to be less impetuous, less emotional, she wrote. But, she warned, "I must love and admire with warmth, or I sink into sadness."

Traveling had stopped her dangerous descent into morbid self-pity. But at last she began to miss her own home. She missed the sophistication of Paris and London. The rugged roads that wound through pine forests were still charming, she wrote, and the sudden roar of water descending from dark cavities in bare rocks was sublime. But living here, was to be "bastilled" by nature. She wanted to go home. Yet to what? She dreaded to return to her solitary lodging, where again she must close her eyes on a world in which, she wrote, "I was destined to wander alone."

The solitary wanderer, as she called herself, with Fanny and Marguerite in tow, arrived in London in October 1795. She was a seasoned traveler who could manage on her own both in a strange land, however threatening the rocks, and on strange seas, however perilous the water. "I enter a boat with the same indifference as I change horses," she fairly boasted. It was amusing to study Marguerite's excitement at her travels now that she had survived seasickness and fear of brigands and cutthroats. As her maid proudly displayed her collection of coins from Scandinavia, Wollstonecraft turned her thoughts to Imlay and the slim hopes she cherished that he was, after all, the kind and good American frontiersman she had met in Paris.

Face to face with Imlay again, she could not sustain any illusions. He acknowledged frankly that he had set up a house for the actress from the strolling theater company. Perhaps, Mary suggested, she could live with Imlay and this woman together. This was a dreadful reprise of the proposal she had made to Sophia Fuseli. Wollstonecraft claimed she hoped that at least Fanny and Imlay would learn to love each other. Imlay wavered, but the actress rejected the proposal. Humiliated, Wollstonecraft gave up hope that she could recover from her misery. To go on living seemed again too hard. She had hauled herself out of despair before and had many times fought away crippling melancholy. But this time she meant to end her life and to do the job well.

She left a note for Imlay and wrote out plans for Fanny's care. On a rainy October morning she walked to Battersea Bridge, then in grim, low marshland in south London. Because there were people about who might intervene, she rented a boat, proud of the rowing skills she had learned in Scandinavia, and went upriver toward Putney. It was still raining. With the boat moored out of sight, she walked up and down the bridge for a half hour to make sure that her clothes were heavy with rainwater, and so more likely to sink. At last she climbed up on the railings and jumped into the Thames.

Despite her efforts, Wollstonecraft's long skirts billowed and kept her afloat. She tried to press the cloth down against her body, and waited to lose consciousness. Meanwhile, some boatmen had seen her fall and came to her rescue. They pulled her senseless from the water and took her to a nearby tavern, where they called in a doctor to revive her. At first no one knew who this half-drowned woman was. But somehow identification was made. In physical and mental misery, Wollstonecraft went to the Christies to be nursed back to health. The physical pain of her attempted suicide was so great, she vowed never to act so desperately again.

Like a bad dream, the sad affair with Gilbert Imlay moved slowly to its final scene. In February 1796, when Imlay returned to London from a trip to Paris, the former lovers met again at the Christies. It was an unplanned, awkward meeting. When Wollstonecraft entered the drawing room with Fanny, Mrs. Christie met her at the front door and advised her to turn away. But taking Fanny with her, Wollstonecraft confronted the child's father. Why should she hang back, she reasoned, from facing someone who had injured her?

They left together and talked, but finally Wollstonecraft accepted what Imlay had known for some time: They would never make a home together. Later, she wrote him one last letter. "It is strange that, in spite of all you do, something like conviction forces me to believe, that you are not what you appear to be. I part with you in peace." There was one final meeting, again by chance, on the road to London. Imlay was on horseback, and Wollstonecraft was returning from a visit to one of her friends. They stopped to talk, then parted. Wollstonecraft marveled that he meant so little to her. This disease had ended. To the end of her life, Wollstonecraft never allowed friends to speak ill of Imlay. But her love for him had burned out at long last.

"THE MOST EXTRAORDINARY MARRIED PAIR"

In 1796 the philosopher William Godwin was a 40-year-old bachelor, regular and temperate in his habits, and apt to fall asleep in company if he stayed out beyond 11:00 P.M. Sometime in January he picked up Mary Wollstonecraft's latest publication, *Letters Written During a Short Residence in Sweden, Norway, and Denmark*. He was familiar with the author and her best-known work, *A Vindication of the Rights of Woman*. In fact, he had found many of her arguments convincing, since he himself believed that education shaped the moral character of human beings, and that rank and privilege were the source of social misery. But he was not entirely pleased by the *Vindication*. The tone of the writing seemed "rugged" and "harsh" to him, and the grammar was careless. Moreover, he remembered meeting Wollstonecraft at Joseph Johnson's house when he had come to meet Thomas Paine. She had talked all night and argued with him. Godwin had suspected she spoke derisively about him when he was not there. Privately, he thought she was fiery and ill-tempered. He did not expect to like *Letters* when he picked it up, but to his surprise he did. Later, he wrote, "If ever there was a book calculated to make a man in love with its author, this appears to me to be the book."

Godwin was not alone. No work of Wollstonecraft's received such immediate and almost uncontested praise. The reviewer for Joseph Johnson's journal *Analytical Review* wrote that her letters were so "replete with correctness of remark, delicacy of feeling, and pathos of expression, that they will cease to exist only with the language in which they are written." On a trip to London, Robert Southey, one of the younger poets, wrote to a friend, "Have you met with Mary Wollstonecraft's *Letters from Sweden and Norway*? She has made me in love with a cold climate, and frost and snow, with a northern moonlight."

There were good reasons for the warm response to Wollstonecraft's work. At the time Wollstonecraft was writing, literary taste was being shaped by new conventions. Younger poets, such as Southey, William Wordsworth, and later John Keats and Percy Bysshe Shelley, were turning away from the elegant formality of Enlightenment literature in favor of more spontaneous responses to the natural world. Rapture and ecstacy, or melancholia and morbidity—all moods were interesting so long as they seemed genuine. William Wordsworth, the young Romantic poet, called poetry "emotion recollected in tranquility." Emotion mattered, believed these young writers. Reason and the mind were not the only avenues to truth.

The figure of Wollstonecraft as a melancholy, solitary traveler made the *Letters* irresistible to readers. She was a genius, an artist—and unhappy. The combination seemed not only plausible, but appealing and appropriate. She had recorded her impressions of Scandinavia by the light of the midnight sun and had poured out her heart's longings in letters to the callow Imlay.

Philosopher and political reformer William Godwin condemned all forms of government and urged reasonable men and women to be each other's caretakers. When in 1796 he was invited to renew his acquaintance with the famous author of A Vindication of the Rights of Woman, *he recalled without pleasure that "she has frequently amused herself by depreciating me."*

Then, once she was back in London, and even while her life seemed a misery to her, she retrieved her letters from him, assembled her notes, and put them in manuscript form for Johnson.

Meeting Wollstonecraft in the pages of the *Letters,* William Godwin was smitten. "She speaks of her sorrows in a way that fills us with melancholy and dissolves us in tenderness, at the same time that she displays a genius which commands all our admiration." Other travel literature had suppressed the personality of the narrating traveler. In Wollstonecraft's *Letters,* however, readers loved the sad reflections and spirited opinions of this young mother addressing her absent lover.

The younger poets hailed her as one of their own. Rumors of her unrequited love for Imlay and her desperate plunge into the Thames made her even more interesting. While visiting London, Robert Southey became enraptured with Wollstonecraft. "Of all the [faces of] lions or literati that I have seen here," he reported, Wollstonecraft's was "the best." Southey loved her light brown eyes and forgave her the slight assumption of superiority that he detected in her manner.

Godwin met Wollstonecraft again in January 1796, at the home of a mutual friend, Mary Hays, about the same time he read her *Letters.* He had not wanted to come to tea. Wollstonecraft, he believed, disliked him. But he did not believe in holding grudges, and he came. There was, he thought, something mournful about Wollstonecraft in the flesh, that quite displaced the disagreeable woman he remembered. Everyone in Johnson's circle had heard about Imlay and probably about Fuseli as well. Only a few months earlier she had made the attempt on her own life. Godwin felt a quiet sympathy for Wollstonecraft's all-too-apparent anguish. By the end of the visit, Godwin and Wollstonecraft no longer disliked each other.

He had reason to be confident about himself. By now William Godwin was a formidable man who had an impressive intellectual and literary reputation. Progressive thinkers admired the brave stand he had taken a few years earlier during the treason trials of the London Corresponding Society.

In 1793 while Wollstonecraft was in Paris, Godwin had published his great work, *An Enquiry Concerning Political Justice,* in which he condemned all governments as artificial, even unnecessary, structures. As Wollstonecraft's *Vindication* was the first important feminist argument, Godwin's *Enquiry* was the first extended argument for anarchism. Godwin believed that if people would live rationally, they could be one another's guardians and thus prevent the behaviors that justified laws. A year after he published this work, while critics of the government were cowed into silence by the reprisals of Pitt's anti-sedition laws, Godwin courageously had come forward to defend his friends John Horne Tooke and Thomas Holcroft, who were on trial for treason.

William Godwin (right) gave support to his friend Thomas Holcroft (left), who was tried for treason in London in 1794. The anti-French hysteria in London had been so whipped up by the government that Holcroft and his peaceful fellow members of a political reform society were called "the meanest and most despicable of people," who were corrupted by "the monstrous doctrine of the Rights of Man."

Godwin's ringing defense of the right to dissent was broadcast all over London in an anonymous letter to a newspaper. However, since any government agent could have traced the letter back to him, Godwin easily might have been the next victim of Pitt's repression and been dispatched to a harsh penal colony at Botany Bay in Australia for punishment. Instead, his words changed public opinion and brought in a verdict of "innocent" for Tooke and Holcroft. For some time Godwin was the toast of radical London society.

Still, there was something slightly fussy about Godwin. The regularity of his daily habits was painstaking and particular. Every morning before breakfast he read for two hours. Then he read and wrote until it was time for his midday meal. In the afternoon he visited or received visitors. In the evening before retiring he carefully wrote in his diary.

Godwin, unlike Imlay, did not cut a dashing figure. Robert Southey, thought he had a comical nose, which he longed to pull off. "—oh, the most abominable nose!" cried Southey. "Language is not vituperatious enough to describe the effect of its downward elongation." But Godwin's eyes were large and impressive, he conceded, somewhat like Fuseli's. And Godwin's company was pleasant. He easily commanded the attentions of several important women, such as Sarah Siddons, the great tragic actress; playwright Elizabeth Inchbald; and Amelia Alderson, the young writer who was famous for crossing the courtroom and kissing Tooke when he was acquitted of treason.

During the winter months that followed Mary Hays's tea party, Wollstonecraft visited friends outside of London. When she returned, she made decisions about how she would live. Perhaps she would travel to Italy and Switzerland, but not immediately. She was writing book reviews and doing editorial work for Johnson again, and money was coming in slowly. Although Imlay had promised to help support Fanny, he had sent nothing. She would wait, save money, and then perhaps build a life for herself and her child abroad, where growing up fatherless with an unmarried mother would be easier for Fanny.

Meanwhile, Mary distanced herself from the neighborhood around Christie's house, where memories of so much unhappiness lingered. She, Marguerite, and Fanny moved into furnished rooms in Pentonville, then an attractive, almost rural northern suburb of London. Most of her old furniture was still in storage. When she looked about her, little was familiar. The Barlows had left England, and Thomas Christie had died that year while traveling in the Far East. Even dear old Joseph Johnson was subdued now, discouraged by Pitt's repressive laws from convening the welcoming dinners at his home near St. Paul's. None of her family was nearby, except Ned whom she disliked. Charles was in the United States, James was at sea, Eliza never wrote, and Everina was in Ireland. Her father, not improved by age, lived on and on in Wales.

But the Pentonville neighborhood was home to someone she knew slightly and did not mind meeting again. One spring day in 1796 Mary Wollstonecraft walked a short distance from her furnished rooms and knocked on the door of William Godwin. Women did not usually call upon men unannounced, and

Godwin was startled to see her. How like her, he thought later, not to be bound by silly conventions. In his diary that night he wrote simply, "Wollstonecraft calls." Later, writing about this time in their lives, Godwin said, "it was friendship melting into love."

Friendship it certainly was. In *A Vindication of the Rights of Woman* Wollstonecraft had claimed that no higher and more exalted relationship than this should build the foundation of a happy home. "Friend Godwin," she called him when she was feeling affectionate. As the summer began, they shaped the character of their developing companionable romance. They would be intellectual and passionate, respectful of each other's privacy, candid, affectionate, and loyal. Both writers, they shared a fondness for correspondence. Marguerite, with Fanny in tow, walked back and forth between their two households, carrying newspapers, books, meals, and hastily scribbled notes that announced plans, gave and accepted invitations to dinner, and mended quarrels.

It was a pleasant household that Wollstonecraft gathered about herself in Pentonville. In early summer 1796, when she moved into larger rooms, collected her old furniture from storage, and added Lucas the cat to her family, Wollstonecraft was acknowledging that she might reside in London for a while longer. She hired two servants to help her. Now she was not continually caring for her darling Fanny, nor having to shop, make the fire, sweep the floor, and mend the linen. There was time to write, and to meet new people.

Through her friendship with Godwin, her circle of acquaintances broadened to include important people working in the arts, such as the actress Sarah Siddons and the playwright Elizabeth Inchbald. Mrs. Siddons's scholarly brother-in-law Francis Twiss and his wife frequently asked Wollstonecraft to dinner. Happily, at 37 she was old enough now to attract the attention of disciples, among them the enterprising writer Mary Hays, who sent Wollstonecraft her manuscripts for criticism, and the vivacious young Amelia Alderson. Alderson teased that she had been in "awe" of the philosopher who had

Sarah Siddons, acknowledged queen of the stage in her lifetime, sat for some of the great portrait painters of the day, including Joshua Reynolds and Thomas Gainsborough. This engraving was made from a Gainsborough painting.

125

written *Vindication* but was now prepared to love the writer of the travel letters from Scandinavia.

There was time for dinner with new friends, such as the political radicals John Horne Tooke and Thomas Holcroft; time to meet some of Godwin's friends, including the brilliant poet George Dyson; and time to spend evenings at the theater. Wollstonecraft also found time to cross London at intervals to meet with her old friend and employer, Joseph Johnson, or to keep up her friendship with Mrs. Christie.

She had always been good company. Now she was an acknowledged member of the "literati," as Southey proclaimed her. When the actor John Kemble gave a dinner party in her honor and invited other luminaries, including Elizabeth Inchbald, playwright Richard Brinsley Sheridan and the great Irish judge and courtroom orator John Curran, the conversation turned to love. London never seemed so splendid to the younger poets coming down from university. As William Hazlitt wrote, "What a subject! What Speakers and what would I not give to have been here." When Godwin and one of his friends, Basil Montagu, took Wollstonecraft for a carriage ride in the country, Amelia Alderson exclaimed, "How I envy the horses. . . . Two Antonys and a Cleopatra."

Stimulated by companionship, and needing money, Wollstonecraft was working on a novel she was titling *Maria*. In this work she wanted to describe the oppression of women from two different social classes. With Godwin nearby, she had found an interested reader and sent him pages of the manuscript as she wrote them. Wollstonecraft was not happy with her work. She thought *Maria* was a "crude production," as she called it later in a letter she wrote to Everina. She never finished the novel and never had many literary expectations for it. But as Fanny helped carry pages of the manuscript down the street to Godwin, Wollstonecraft shared with her new friend the memories of her childhood and the crises of her adult life that she was incorporating into her novel. These exchanges were the first tentative steps toward intimacy.

So began a happier period of Mary Wollstonecraft's life. Godwin and Wollstonecraft were indeed temperamentally dissimilar, but their shared lives as writers and political sympathies provided a strong ground from which they could take stock of each other. Moreover neither one was still young. As such, they were more tolerant and wiser than they might have been earlier in their lives, and understood themselves, their failures, their strengths, and their desires. Nor was either one of them shy about appraising the other.

Godwin thought Wollstonecraft's writing was rough and ungrammatical. She heard him out but would not yield to him completely. Instead, she defended her "effusions of feelings," which she prized above the "cold workings of the brain." On her part, she wished he were less careful and more imaginative. He wished she were sometimes less emotional, and cautioned her that her feelings tyrannized over her.

As the summer of 1796 wore on, Fanny and Marguerite carried notes back and forth more and more frequently, along with books and manuscripts. Sometimes the little messenger was rewarded with cookies, as Wollstonecraft was also teaching Godwin how to be an affectionate member of her household. "Give Fanny a biscuit," she wrote to him in notes attached to the daily newspapers. "I want you to love each other." Later, other instructions for Fanny's diet came down the street with the daily notes. "Don't give Fanny cake," or "Don't give Fanny butter with her pudding."

Godwin claimed to be unhappy when his daily newspaper arrived without Fanny as the deliverer. He heard about the progress of her chicken pox, learned to recognize her baby talk, and found a perfect initialed mug for her at the pottery factory of his friend Josiah Wedgwood outside of London.

Wollstonecraft was willing to criticize his writing as well. In July Godwin sent her a love poem, which she pronounced flawed because he did not examine his own heart. Tell me your feelings, she insisted. He did. "Your company infinitely delights me," he wrote, adding, "I love your imagination." He loved "the malicious leer" of her eye, "in short everything that constitutes the bewitching tout ensemble of the celebrated Mary."

The "celebrated Mary" had at last found a faithful friend. But she was a while convincing herself she could depend on him. Godwin had, after all, other admirers; and in the first months of their growing regard for each other, Wollstonecraft took note of his opinions of these other women with mild anxiety disguised as wit. Elizabeth Inchbald she called "Mrs. Perfection," teasing Godwin that he preferred her company.

Amelia Alderson might have been more serious competition. Godwin had been courting her when Wollstonecraft became his neighbor. But at 27 Alderson found Godwin bashful as a suitor and rejected his half-hearted proposal of marriage as not being serious. Wollstonecraft and Alderson became friends, and once Wollstonecraft learned of Godwin's proposal, she teased him about his alleged rapture. "Miss Alderson was wondering this morning whether you *ever* kissed a maiden fair," she wrote to Godwin. She addressed her envelope to "Willm Godwin Philosopher," adding "Not to be opened 'till the Philosopher has been an hour at least in Miss Alderson's company, cheek by jowl."

Godwin did not always know how to respond to the quick play of moods of his "bewitching" Mary. He wrote her that he could not always tell when she was joking and when she was serious. When she wanted to tease him, she called him "profound Grammarian" or "Your Philosophership"; when she was angry or hurt, she called his philosophy "icy." The sudden alterations of her feelings alarmed and disturbed him. But they never drove him from her.

In August they reached a moment of crisis. Wollstonecraft could not accept the fact that she had entered into a new intimacy without some panic. Desolate that she might be deceived and abandoned again, she wrote coldly to Godwin that he had abused her confidence in him, "acted injudiciously," and, full of his own feelings, forgot hers. She was, she wrote, "mortified" and "humbled," and would pack up and disappear with Fanny into another, distant country "in a twinkle" if only she could. Remembering, and quoting from, her travel *Letters from Scandinavia,* she wrote, "I will become a solitary walker."

But William Godwin was not Gilbert Imlay. Even in her most chilling and angry posture, Wollstonecraft could not weary Godwin or make him feel trapped. He understood the crisis of confidence that prompted her letter and he addressed himself to this anxiety at once. "I see nothing in you but what I respect and adore," he wrote. "Do not hate me. Indeed I do not deserve it. Do not cast me off. Do not become again a solitary walker."

Reassured, she wrote back quickly, inviting Godwin to dinner. But she was again vulnerable to doubts and anxieties. Two days later she wrote a lengthy letter to him, describing a walk she had taken with Fanny that morning. She had come upon a poor sycamore tree whose young branches were being beaten back by winds. The tree mistook a sunny day in early winter for spring, and now its buds were blasted by frost. The story might have come from *Original Stories,* the book of instructive tales for children she had written years earlier. This time she was instructing William Godwin. She was that sycamore, she implied. Was Godwin that false spring?

"I have no answer to make to your fable," he replied. "I see not . . . its application." He wished for reassurance too. "I need soothing," he complained. "You threaten me."

"I am sometimes humble," she replied. "Write me but a line, just to assure me, that you have been thinking of me with affection, now and then—since we parted."

"Humble," he protested. "For heaven's sake, be proud, be arrogant! You are—but I cannot tell what you are. I cannot yet find the circumstance about you that allies you to the frailty of our nature. I will hunt it out."

As they were learning to know each other, the careful housekeeping the couple shared, while maintaining their own separate residences, was often sweet. Godwin claimed Wollstonecraft was a "worshipper of domestic life." Indeed, she told him it was pleasant to send him his household linen, to feel entitled to ask for his keys. When Godwin reached for her hand while they were out with friends, she told him she was more "gratified than I could have been by all the admiration in the world, tho' I am a woman—and to mount a step higher in the scale of vanity, an author."

At Christmastime Wollstonecraft realized that she was pregnant. She suffered the nausea of early pregnancy, an "inelegant complaint," as she called it in a letter to Godwin. "It is very tormenting to be thus, neither sick nor well." Godwin was reassuring. Wollstonecraft wrote, "There was a tenderness in your manner as you seemed to be opening your heart to a new born affection, that rendered you very dear to me." Still, the pregnancy raised problems for the couple. They had kept their developing romance a secret from their friends. They must now announce to the world that they had formed an intimate relationship.

In fact, most people believed that Mary Wollstonecraft was Mary Imlay. Although she published *Letters from Scandinavia* under her familiar author's name "Wollstonecraft," she signed letters to friends as "Mary Imlay." She told Godwin that she used Imlay's name because it might make Fanny's life easier. But Wollstonecraft was candid with friends. She told them that she and Imlay had not been legally married. Still, many of her more conventional friends preferred to maintain the fiction that Wollstonecraft and Imlay were married, although no longer living together.

Wollstonecraft and Godwin were quiet about their plans to marry and did not share them with Everina when she came to visit for some weeks in February 1797. Everina was, as always, an unamusing houseguest, and her visit was not improved when she caught a bad winter cold and had to remain indoors. When Godwin visited in the evening, Everina sat among them stonily and conversation faltered. "A little patience," Wollstonecraft advised Godwin, although they both yearned for her visitor to leave. When Everina at last departed to take up a post as governess to the Wedgwood family, friends of Godwin's, she left behind some face powder and some unpaid bills, which Wollstonecraft paid.

Problems about money loomed large. Although Godwin hoped that as successful authors they would earn enough income, he had never saved the kind of

money a family might need. Even more worrisome, as Wollstonecraft's husband, he would become responsible for her debts. She had borrowed liberally from Joseph Johnson, who would now expect payment from Godwin. This possible embarrassment was reason enough to delay the wedding until they had earned more money.

William Godwin and Mary Wollstonecraft married on March 29, 1797. It was a quiet ceremony at St. Pancras Parish Church in north London. They made little of the moment. In fact, Godwin did not even mention the event in his diary. But the marriage astounded both their radical and their more conservative friends. The more conservative ones were now forced to accept that Wollstonecraft was never married to Gilbert Imlay. Sarah Siddons, the actress, and her relatives the scholarly Twisses, cut them at once. Elizabeth Inchbald, who had always been jealous, sent them a withering note and withdrew her theater invitations. "I most sincerely wish you and Mrs. Godwin joy," she wrote. "But, assured that your joyfulness would obliterate from memory every trifling engagement, I have entreated another person to supply your place and perform your office in securing a box on Reynold's night. If I have done wrong, when you next marry, I will act differently."

Their more radical friends were surprised and then vastly amused. Godwin had, after all, railed against marriage in his philosophical works. Marriage was, he had maintained, an artificial bond that two virtuous people should neither desire nor require. Wollstonecraft had never disagreed with this statement. She had been proud that she had never sworn obedience to

Mary Wollstonecraft and William Godwin recorded their marriage to each other in March 1797 at St. Pancras Church in London. Passing on the news to a friend, Godwin wrote, "We found that there was no way so obvious for her to drop the name of Imlay, as to assume the name of Godwin, Mrs. Godwin—who the devil is that?"

any man. Their old friend Henry Fuseli laughed when he heard the news. "The *assertrix* of female rights has given her hand to the *balancier* of political justice," he proclaimed.

Godwin explained his actions somewhat pompously to a friend. "Nothing but a regard for the happiness of the individual, which I had no right to injure, could have induced me to submit to an institution which I wish to see abolished, and which I would recommend to my fellow-men, never to practise, but with the greatest caution." He added that he felt himself to be no more differently "bound" than he was before the ceremony. Moreover, he reassured his friend, "we do not entirely cohabit."

There were some well-wishers. Thomas Holcroft was jubilant. "From my very heart and soul I wish you joy," he wrote. "I think you are the most extraordinary married pair in existence." Godwin's mother wished them happiness. The pious old woman had raised her son to be a minister and was disappointed when he gave up his faith. Mrs. Godwin wrote to her son, saying she hoped that since he had changed his mind about marriage, perhaps too he would be restored to religion. Meanwhile, she sent him a small feather bed, big enough for a servant, and some eggs, which she advised him to keep on sawdust or bran and turn often so they wouldn't spoil.

Mrs. Godwin would have been startled by her son and daughter-in-law's living arrangements. Indeed, as Godwin had said, they did not entirely cohabit. They shared a house in Somers Town, then an agreeable London neighborhood for artists and literary people. Yet Godwin kept a room as a study across the street and maintained his old bachelor habits of writing there for a few hours in the morning before breakfast. Often he slept there as well, and the couple would not meet until dinnertime, unless they chanced to see each other while out walking.

Wollstonecraft and Godwin were determined to show the world they could marry without losing their independence. They both disapproved of the widespread belief that husband

and wife must go out socially only in each other's company. They meant to see their mutual friends as individuals. Godwin continued to disapprove of marriage in principle. Early that summer as he traveled in the country with Basil Montagu, he wrote Wollstonecraft, telling her that his friend might propose marriage to a daughter of the Wedgwoods. In his letter Godwin wrote, "I look upon any of my friends going to be married with something of the feeling as I should do if they were sentenced to hard labour. . . . The despot may die and the new despot grace his accession with a general jail delivery; that is almost the only hope for the unfortunate captive."

Wollstonecraft was not at all alarmed by such sentiments. Throughout her professional life she had claimed that the institution of marriage either oppressed women directly or smothered exceptional women who might be more usefully engaged outside of housekeeping. Now she protested to her friends that marriage would in no way compromise her integrity. "It is my wish that Mr. Godwin should visit and dine out as formerly and I shall do the same," she wrote to Amelia Alderson.

Furthermore, she claimed, she meant to raise her children according to her own beliefs, even if Godwin disagreed with her. She might have married any number of wealthy or important people, she wrote to Alderson, except that she insisted on someone "with similar pursuits, bound to me by affection." Wollstonecraft would not forgive Elizabeth Inchbald for her disagreeable congratulations, and she mocked her savagely to friends. But she was sorry to lose the friendship of the Twisses, whom she respected. Still, she affirmed, "my conduct in life must be directed by my own judgment and moral principles."

Wollstonecraft and Godwin were faithful to the principle that they should lead independent lives and, as much as possible, continued to meet their own friends on social occasions without each other. One of their quarrels arose in June when they met each other unexpectedly at dinner at Thomas Holcroft's. Since he had invited them both, who should have accepted the

MARY WOLLSTONECRAFT TO WILLIAM GODWIN

Wollstonecraft and Godwin were separated briefly after their marriage when Godwin traveled into the countryside to visit a friend. They were anticipating the birth of their baby, whom they imagined as a son named for his father, William. New to married life, Wollstonecraft teased Godwin about their shared conviction that they should not always have to be in each other's company.

[London] June 6, 1797

I was not quite well the day after you left me; but it is past, and I am well and tranquil, excepting the disturbance produced by Master William's joy, who took it into his head to frisk a little at being informed of your remembrance. I begin to love this little creature, and to anticipate his birth as a fresh twist to a knot, which I do not wish to untie. Men are spoilt by frankness, I believe, yet I must tell you that I love you for ever—and I will add what will gratify your benevolence, if not your heart, that on the whole I may be termed happy. You are a tender, affectionate creature; and I feel it thrilling through my frame giving and promising pleasure . . .

I find you can write the kind of letter a friend ought to write, and give an account of your movements. I hailed the sunshine, and moon-light and travelled with you scenting the fragrant gale—Enable me still to be your company, and I will allow you to peep over my shoulder, and see me under the shade of my green blind, thinking of you, and all I am to hear, and feel when you return—you may read my heart—if you will . . .

I am not fatigued with solitude—yet I have not relished my solitary dinner. A husband is a convenient part of the furniture of a home, unless he be a clumsy fixture. I wish you, from my soul, to be rivetted in my heart; but I do not desire to have you always at my elbow—though at this moment I did not care if you were.

invitation? Godwin believed that since he was Holcroft's friend before Wollstonecraft was, the right to attend the dinner was his. Wollstonecraft agreed with him "in principle," but perhaps not in this situation. She was unable to explain why this situation was different, though, and dropped the discussion.

There were also compensations for the married state. Wollstonecraft felt able to turn over to Godwin the disagreeable business of negotiating with tradesmen and landlords. She hated worrying about sinks and paying overdue bills. "My time appears to me as valuable as that of any other person accustomed to employ themselves," she told Godwin, who did not raise the traditional argument that paying the baker and unclogging the sink was women's work.

Meanwhile, Wollstonecraft was still working on her novel *Maria*. She sketched plans for its completion, but found the work vexing. Godwin's friend George Dyson read her manuscript for her. He and Godwin were full of useful suggestions, but when Dyson complained that Maria's predicament didn't seem to justify her flight from her husband, Wollstonecraft protested that indeed it did. Maria was a "woman of sensibility with an improving mind," who was married to a thick-skinned cad. If Dyson could not understand, she suggested, the reason must be that he is a man.

While she awaited the birth of her second child, Wollstonecraft was also working on a lesson book for small children. She had adopted a narrative form, addressing her remarks to Fanny, whom she imagined now as the older sister of a little brother named William. "When you were a baby, with no more sense than William, you put everything into your mouth. . . . See how much taller you are than William. In four years, you have learned to eat, to work, to talk."

Little unborn William was very real to her. She and Godwin had been playfully imagining this child as a boy. Godwin had ended a long letter to Wollstonecraft, saying he "salutes the trio, M., F, and last and least (in stature at least) little W." But it was not little William, after all, who arrived on August 30.

Wollstonecraft wrote to Godwin at his study early in the day that she expected the birth. "I have no doubt of seeing the animal today," she wrote, using the simple affectionate term that was often used to describe small babies. She was waiting for the midwife, Mrs. Blenkinsop, and asked Godwin to send over a newspaper, or a novel, or anything amusing that she might read.

Mrs. Blenkinsop was practiced in the age-old skill of delivering babies. Godwin agreed with Wollstonecraft's preference for a midwife rather than a doctor, unless problems arose. At first there seemed to be no problems. Godwin had dinner with friends and went back to his study to wait for his child to be born. Wollstonecraft asked him to stay away until the baby had arrived. When Godwin came to their shared home after dinner, he stayed downstairs. Shortly before midnight, Mary Godwin was born.

But all was not well. Sometime later Mrs. Blenkinsop came down in alarm and asked Godwin to fetch a doctor. He rushed to the nearby Westminster hospital and brought a doctor back with him. But there was little the doctor could do. Because there was no knowledge of how bacteria spread, medical practices were woefully deficient in antiseptic procedures. Mary Wollstonecraft had contracted a massive infection called "childbed fever."

She lingered for days. Anxious friends visited, and she took nourishment from Godwin in spoonfuls. But finally, on Sunday, September 10, shortly after dawn, Mary Wollstonecraft died. Godwin, overwhelmed, could record no more than the day and time in his journal.

Godwin was left to care for an infant and a small girl, without the companionship and love of the woman who had entered his life a year and a half earlier and transformed it. "This light," he wrote in his memoirs of Wollstonecraft, "was lent to me for a very short period, and is now extinguished forever!"

Mary Wollstonecraft wrote optimistic notes to Godwin while awaiting her baby's birth, preferring Godwin remain in his study across the street until he was called. She expected the birth to be easy and that she would come down for dinner the next day, but, as Godwin wrote in his memoirs, "she went up to her chamber,—never more to descend."

"WITHOUT A TEAR": THE LEGACY OF MARY WOLLSTONECRAFT

William Godwin could not be consoled. "I have not the least expectation," he wrote to Thomas Holcroft, "that I can now ever know happiness again." He arranged a small, quiet funeral and invited a few close friends, but he was finally too stricken to attend. Mary Wollstonecraft was buried in the tree-shaded yard outside St. Pancras Parish Church. Alongside the stone tablet that Godwin erected, he planted two weeping willows.

The sad news of Wollstonecraft's death traveled across London. Joseph Johnson wrote to Godwin, saying that even while he was receiving discouraging reports of Mary's decline, he still hoped that her natural physical strength would help her rally. Johnson wrote to Wollstonecraft's old friend Henry Fuseli, "One who loved you, and whom I respected, is no more." Fuseli wrote back, "Poor Mary." Friends, sparing Godwin the task, wrote to Everina, asking that she pass on the news to their sister, Eliza. No one heard from Gilbert Imlay.

Several days after the funeral, Godwin moved from his separate rooms into the house he had shared with Wollstonecraft. Suddenly he was responsible for the care of two small girls who were deprived of the parent who knew how to raise them. "The poor children!" he wrote. "I am myself totally unfitted to

*Only months after she
was married there,
Mary Wollstonecraft
was buried at old St.
Pancras Church.
Godwin planted two
weeping willows on
her grave and years
later, at his request,
was buried alongside
her. After railroad
tracks were laid
through the neighbor-
hood in the 19th cen-
tury, Wollstonecraft's
grandson moved their
remains to Bourne-
mouth, but the grave-
marker still stands.*

educate them. . . . She was the best qualified in the world!" After
finding caretakers for Fanny and baby Mary, Godwin turned to
the work he could do well. Placing a portrait of Wollstonecraft
over his desk, he exhausted his sadness in writing her biography.
He asked Everina to send him details of their shared childhood,
but she was cool and uncooperative. When he asked Fuseli for
the letters Wollstonecraft had written him, the artist showed him
drawers filled with her letters and yelled, "That's as close as you'll
get to them, damn you!" Jane Arden sent Godwin all of the girlhood correspondence she had from Mary.

Godwin held little back as he wrote about Wollstonecraft's
life. Although he protected Eliza Bishop by omitting mention
of her flight from an unhappy marriage, he wrote honestly
about Wollstonecraft's admiration for Henry Fuseli, her love
affair with Gilbert Imlay, the birth of Fanny Imlay, and her suicide attempts. He did not conceal that he and Wollstonecraft
had lived together without marrying.

GODWIN ON WOLLSTONECRAFT
AFTER HER DEATH

Grief-stricken, William Godwin wrote a memoir of Wollstonecraft's life shortly after her death, describing the character of her mind and the depth of his loss.

Mary and myself perhaps each carried farther than to its common extent the characteristic of the sexes to which we belonged. I have been stimulated, as long as I can remember, by the love of intellectual distinction; but, as long as I can remember, I have been discouraged, when casting the sum of my intellectual value, by finding that I did not possess, in the degree of some other persons, an intuitive sense of the pleasures of the imagination.

What I wanted in this respect, Mary possessed in a degree superior to any other person I ever knew. Her feelings had a character of peculiar strength and decision; and the discovery of them, whether in matters of taste or of moral virtue, she found herself unable to control. She had viewed the objects of nature with a lively sense and an ardent admiration, and had developed their beauties . . .

A companion like this, excites and animates the mind . . . Her taste awakened mine; her sensibility determined me to a careful development of my feelings. She delighted to open her heart to the beauties of nature; and her propensity in this respect led me to a more intimate contemplation of them . . .

The improvement I had reason to promise myself, was however yet in its commencement, when a fatal event, hostile to the moral interests of mankind, ravished from me the light of my steps, and left nothing but the consciousness of what I had possessed, and must now possess no more!

Godwin in his later years never recovered the brilliance of his earlier writing. Publishing unimportant novels and essays to meet constant debts, Godwin cut a sorry figure, grown "quite juvenile," said a contemporary, smiling pointlessly, wriggling, with "more affectation than a canary bird pluming his feathers."

When Johnson published Godwin's memoirs in 1798, a startled public read about her unconventional life. This was the same British readership to which Wollstonecraft had so reluctantly returned three years earlier. She was uneasy then about the mood of political repression that pervaded her native land. At the time her biography was published, opinion in Britain was still being shaped by reactions to the French Revolution. Any practice that challenged conventional morality was heard as the clang of the French tocsin calling out the mob to rebellion. In the minds of many who read Godwin's description of Wollstonecraft's life, her unmarried motherhood, her suicidal despair, and her argument for the rights of women were blurred. Feminism, these people reasoned, led to misery. One journal went so far as to cross-reference Mary Wollstonecraft's name with "prostitution" in the index to its essays.

Even sympathetic friends wondered why Godwin had been so candid. Wollstonecraft's weaknesses should have been buried in oblivion, suggested reviewers, rather than waved under the noses of Britain's reading public. Only Joseph Johnson's press was kind. "We have no fellowship," he argued, with anyone who could read the memoirs "without a tear."

Few people were willing to defend the life of Mary Wollstonecraft, and far fewer were willing to continue with the work of improving society so that women could lead full intellectual, political, and emotional lives. Wollstonecraft's friend Mary Hays did come forward, publishing an *Appeal to the Men of Great Britain in Behalf of the Women* a year after Wollstonecraft's death. But Hays's call for the reform of legal barriers to women's advancement was ignored or dismissed. A more appealing work to many was Maria Edgeworth's essay, *Practical Education,* published the same year. It advised girls to be passive, to "adapt themselves to what is."

It appeared as if interest in women's rights had died with Mary Wollstonecraft. In the years following her death, Hannah More, a conservative opponent of the French Revolution, wrote pamphlets for Pitt's government to discourage political unrest in the English countryside. More viciously attacked Wollstonecraft as being immoral, and argued that women had no part to play in public affairs. Years earlier, when the *Vindication* was first published, More had written mockingly about Mary Wollstonecraft's essay on women's rights, claiming that there was something so ridiculous in the title, she would not read the work. Now More had Godwin's memoirs of Wollstonecraft to support her claim that a woman who argued for her rights would bring only misery upon herself and the other unhappy people who depended on her.

When he had finished his writing, Godwin set himself the task of making a home for the two girls, Fanny and baby Mary. Several years after Wollstonecraft's death, he provided them with a stepmother by marrying Mary Jane Clairmont, a widow with a son and daughter. But their home life was not particularly happy. Godwin grew into a nervous older fatherhood, worrying about money, while his two daughters felt they had no reason to be fond of their stepmother. Fanny Imlay, the merry baby of Wollstonecraft's travels, became a quiet child, anxious to please, and grew up in the shadow of her much-loved younger sister, Mary. Unfortunately, Fanny inherited her mother's tendency toward melancholia without inheriting her capacity for recovery. Nor was it easy for her to be known as the daughter of the scandalous Mary Wollstonecraft and the negligent lover Gilbert Imlay.

Her younger sister had an easier time. At her birth, family friends pronounced that the measurements of Mary Godwin's head promised great intelligence. Godwin, claiming objectivity, felt that his daughter was both more beautiful and more brilliant than her older sister Fanny. Mary Godwin grew up close to her father, even as he grew into an eccentric and

Frankenstein awakens into life in the first illustration of Mary Godwin Shelley's famous novel. Dr. Frankenstein planned to create a perfect form of life, but, horrified, he records in his journal, "By the glimmer of the half-extinguished light, I saw the dull yellow eye of the creature open; it breathed hard, and a convulsive motion agitated its limbs."

quarrelsome old man. But when she was 17, Mary Godwin outraged her father by eloping with Percy Bysshe Shelley, the young and politically radical poet. Shelley belonged to the new generation of Romantic poets who had admired Mary Wollstonecraft's writing for its frank expression of noble feelings. According to legend, the two young lovers first met at Mary Wollstonecraft's graveside.

Two years later, in 1814, during a rainy summer in the Swiss Alps with Shelley and the poet Lord Byron, Mary Godwin Shelley wrote the novel *Frankenstein,* perhaps the most famous horror story ever written. In this tale about a deformed man who learns to be evil, she suggests that character is shaped by experience. The monster Frankenstein is not evil at birth; he becomes evil because people treat him badly. Mary Shelley's mother would have approved of her daughter's argument that society is responsible for developing the character of its citizens. Wollstonecraft had argued that women were not naturally ignorant and vain, but rather made so by society.

Meanwhile, with her sister gone, Fanny was alone in her father and stepmother's home. A surprise visit from her mother's old friend George Blood enlivened her temporarily. Blood was visiting London for the first time in 20 years. During his visit to the Godwins, he told Fanny stories about her mother, the friend of his younger days. Fanny was charmed by his reminiscences and wrote to her sister, Mary, "Everything he had told me of my mother has increased my love and admiration of her memory. . . . I have determined never to live to be a disgrace to such a Mother."

For a short while Fanny planned to join her aunts Everina and Eliza in Dublin, where they ran a school, but they withdrew the invitation. Their connection to Mary Wollstonecraft was always embarrassing to them, and now there was the additional scandal of Mary Godwin's elopement with Shelley. Eliza Bishop and Everina Wollstonecraft had to worry about pleasing the parents of prospective students, and so they distanced themselves from the Godwin family.

Fanny had few prospects and no money of her own. She had only a modest legacy left her by Joseph Johnson after his death in 1809.

The writer Mary Godwin Shelley, the second daughter of Mary Wollstonecraft, wrote many works of fiction after the astounding success of her first novel, Frankenstein. *Mary Shelley respected her mother's memory but was not as rebellious. "I am not fond of vindications," she wrote late in life, and prayed for her son, "Oh God, teach him to think like other people."*

Fanny Imlay's resolution to live admirably for her mother's sake was difficult to keep. In 1816, while her sister's novel *Frankenstein* was being published, Fanny traveled alone to Bristol on the west coast of England, perhaps intending to visit her aunts in Ireland. Instead, she sent notes to Godwin and Shelley, warning them that she meant to end her life. The two men rushed to her, but they were too late. Fanny Imlay was already dead. An empty bottle of the drug laudanum lay nearby. In the unsigned note she left, Fanny had written, "I have long determined that the best thing I could do was to put an end to the existence of a being whose birth was unfortunate." Godwin urged that Fanny's wish to die anonymously be respected. She was buried in an unmarked pauper's grave.

After Fanny Imlay's death, Mary Godwin Shelley alone remained to carry Wollstonecraft's legacy into the 19th century. Like her mother, Mary Shelley was left with heavy responsibilities as a young woman. Her husband Shelley drowned in Italy in 1822, leaving her to raise their young son alone. Nor did she receive any adequate allowance from Shelley's father, who disapproved of their elopement and marriage.

Satirists in the late 18th century ridiculed the idea of women's independence and mocked the unladylike character of some women's activities.

Like her mother, Mary Shelley turned to writing to earn her living. But she was warier than Mary Wollstonecraft had been not to offend public opinion. When the women's rights movement stirred faintly into life in her own time, some people naturally turned to Mary Wollstonecraft's daughter for assistance. Mary Shelley's response was guarded. "I am not a person of opinions," she wrote. "On some topics (especially with regard to my own sex), I am far from making up my mind." While she claimed she befriended and assisted any woman who was oppressed, she reminded her friends that she never wrote to vindicate women's rights.

For the most part Mary Wollstonecraft's legacy, an argument for the rights of women, remained unclaimed. Victorian Britain and the United States were as hostile as Wollstonecraft's own time had been to the challenges her life and work implied. Perhaps they were even more so. Increasingly, Wollstonecraft was forgotten. Public sentiment believed that a middle-class woman's place was only in the home, not in public life. Home was the proper place for women whose husbands' incomes were sufficient to keep them there. No one quarreled with the legions of dispossessed poor women, made desperate by the failure of small farms, who left the countryside for the new industrial centers in the northern United States and England. These women, and usually their husbands and children as well, joined the labor forces who were working in the factories. Their lives were remote from the sentimental picture of 19th-century family life that newspapers, magazines, and novels portrayed.

While working-class women toiled, public opinion built a pedestal for middle-class women. Political leaders, ministers, teachers, and writers argued that because the business world was harsh and competitive, a man needed to return in the evenings to a home with a loving woman in it. These shapers of public opinion claimed that virtues such as sweetness, childlike innocence, and unreflecting loyalty naturally belonged to women. Instead of Mary Wollstonecraft's vision of a rational and moral mother or an independent woman earning her own way, 19th-century popular culture nurtured an ideal of woman as angelic and passive. Wollstonecraft's alternative proposal of an educated woman teaching her children according to rational principles was buried under pseudoscientific literature that warned that too much learning would damage a girl's health. Such literature argued that studying classical languages or the sciences might damage the uterus and thus prevent a young girl from having children some day.

While Wollstonecraft's argument was silenced by hostile and contradictory justifications for the subordination of women, different opinions about women's place and women's rights slowly surfaced. In the United States the debate over women's rights emerged again as a consequence of the abolitionist movement. As more people protested that slavery was immoral, reformers argued that women also deserved the full rights of citizenship. Just as Wollstonecraft argued that the rights of man should be extended to women, so too mid-19th-century American reformers issued a call to extend to women the rights won by the American Revolution.

In 1848 a women's rights convention at Seneca Falls, New York, published the Declaration of Sentiments and Resolutions that was modeled on the American Declaration of Independence. "All men and women are created equal [and] endowed by their Creator with certain inalienable rights," pronounced the Seneca Falls conference. Elizabeth Cady Stanton, who drafted the resolutions of the declaration, read these arguments earlier in *A Vindication of the Rights of Woman*.

The Seneca Falls declaration, which launched the women's movement in the United States, claimed women's rights to vote, control property, divorce, retain custody of their own children, and become doctors, lawyers, or ministers, if they wished. Like Mary Wollstonecraft, these women faced scorn, mockery, and denunciation. Some men described with amusement the prospect of women legislators having to interrupt speeches in the halls of Congress because labor pains and childbirth had overcome them. Others predicted that if women voted, the family, already weakened, would disappear. Husband and wife might support different political parties or even be rival candidates for the same political office. Social theorist Orestes Brownson reflected the sentiment for many in 1869 when he preached, "Woman was created to be a wife and a mother. . . . That is her destiny."

Fighting men like Brownson, those who supported women's rights claimed Mary Wollstonecraft's legacy. As the woman suffrage movement gathered force on both sides of the Atlantic, however, its leaders seldom advertised a connection to the author of *A Vindication of the Rights of Woman*. Too heavy a whiff of scandal still clung to Wollstonecraft's memory. The mainstream of the feminist movement, struggling for the vote, hoped to offend as few people as possible by being determinedly respectable.

On one memorable occasion Elizabeth Cady Stanton reminded her audience about Mary Wollstonecraft. Stanton was defending fellow feminist Victoria Woodhull, who was claiming the right to be nominated as President of the United States. Because Woodhull had lived openly with a man outside of marriage, however, the more conservative advocates of women's rights drew back from association with her. Bravely Stanton challenged their Puritanism, arguing, "We have had enough women sacrificed to this sentimental, hypocritical prating about purity. . . . This is one of man's most effective engines for our division and subjugation. He creates the public sentiment, builds the gallows, and then makes us hangmen for our sex. We have crucified the Mary Wollstonecrafts. . . . Let us end this ignoble record. . . . If Victoria Woodhull must be crucified, let men drive the spikes and plait the crown of thorns."

In 1910, academic women marched for the vote in New York, one of many such demonstrations for female suffrage. Some feminists sought more widespread reforms in education and marriage laws and were contemptuous of the movement for the vote, declaring, "the ballot is not even half a loaf; it is only a crust—a crumb."

Elizabeth Cady Stanton's misgivings were important. Indeed, it seemed as if women were marching for the right to vote and for higher education without claiming the right to have and express feelings. The legacy of Mary Wollstonecraft's life and work included her proud refusal to marry only for financial security and her insistence on the inalienable right to love. Early in the 20th century, political radical Emma Goldman, lecturing in New York, called Mary Wollstonecraft "a pioneer of modern womanhood," because she was both intelligent and passionate, an author, a mother, and a lover. To such reformers as Goldman, Wollstonecraft's genius was that she never believed that demanding political rights required her to forsake her claim to a full intellectual and sexual life.

When American women received the vote in 1919, many thought that the battle for women's rights had at last been won. But the celebration was premature. Though higher education was now available to women, prestigious universities were still exclusively male. While women were now legally entitled to control their own property, their ability to earn money was limited because tradition and practice confined professional careers to men. Women voted, but tradition and practice assured that political leaders were men. Still, with the vote won, many assumed that the campaign for women's rights had outlived its usefulness.

In the early part of the 20th century new theories emerged to explain human behavior. These theories argued that feminists were not immoral; rather they were mentally ill. In one work, *Modern Woman: The Lost Sex,* written in 1947, a New York psychiatrist and a sociologist located all that was regrettable about feminism in the personage of Mary Wollstonecraft. Influenced by Sigmund Freud's theories of psychological development, this argument condemned Wollstonecraft not as a philosophic "wanton," as the conservative opponents of the French Revolution had raged, but as a woman who did not like being a woman.

Wollstonecraft was "God's angry woman," claimed these writers. According to them, she wished she were a man and hated men because she envied them.

More than being ridiculed, though, Wollstonecraft was ignored on both sides of the Atlantic as the United States and England recovered from the Second World War. In 1959 the Fawcett Society, advocating women's rights, received a letter from someone in Japan, asking what it was doing to honor the 200th anniversary of Wollstonecraft's birth. No plans had been made, but members of the society dutifully went to her gravestone in London and laid a wreath in her memory.

In the decades between the bicentennial of her birth and the bicentennial of the publication of *A Vindication of the Rights of Woman,* Mary Wollstonecraft was rediscovered. A new generation came to feminism by way of their political engagement in the American civil rights movement of the 1960s. Just as the 19th-century antislavery crusades inspired the Declaration of Sentiments at Seneca Falls, protests to extend civil rights to black Americans heightened the consciousness of young women to the unfinished agendas of the women's rights movement. Raising the banner that "the personal is political," these women examined the work divisions of private life that discouraged women from a full participation in public life.

In their belief that character is shaped by experience, that the ideal of the childlike homebound woman was not natural, but created, feminists evaluated advertisements, movies, television, and prestigious works of literature. Using the same logic that Mary Wollstonecraft employed in *Vindication,* these feminists argued that if the lives of girls were changed, and if society were organized differently, girls would have greater ambitions and a chance to realize them. Wollstonecraft had argued similarly 200 years earlier.

As the feminist movement born of the American civil rights struggle gained strength, it sought its own historical roots and named *A Vindication of the Rights of Woman* as one of its founding texts. In one important review in "The New York Review of Books" of the many new biographies of Wollstonecraft that were published in the early 1970s, she was called the founding mother of feminism.

The founding mother now lies buried in Bournemouth, a seaside resort in southern England. The site of the original grave was destroyed when the great Victorian railroad stations at St. Pancras and King's Cross were erected in London in the mid 19th century. Mary Shelley's son, Sir Percy Shelley, moved his grandmother's grave to the town where he lived. She and William Godwin lie there together.

But the original gravestone Godwin designed still stands in the small churchyard of St. Pancras Parish Church in north London. In 1992, when the women planning the bicentennial celebration of *Vindication* visited the site, they found the stone in a state of decay and neglect. Nearby lay old railroad lines and gas meters. Dismayed that the memory of the mother of feminism was so dishonored, these women publicly urged the restoration of the grave site. The family of undertakers whose forbearers had originally buried Wollstonecraft agreed to restore the grave marker.

It may have been easy to rebuild the stone, but the reforms that Mary Wollstonecraft launched are less easily protected. Francesca Annis, the English actress who read Wollstonecraft's words at her bicentennial celebration said, "I am determined not to stop being a feminist. . . . Feminism has done so much, particularly for a younger generation of women who do not even realize what changes have taken place in our lifetimes."

Mary Wollstonecraft understood that ignorance and indifference erode liberty even faster than time erases granite. Her most important tribute, more longlasting than flowers and kind words, is the continuing campaign for women's rights, a call to arms that her brave writing announced to an astonished world.

CHRONOLOGY

1759
Born April 27 in London

1768
Moves with family to Yorkshire in north England

1773
Begins correspondence with Jane Arden

1775
Moves with family to Hoxton near London; meets Fanny Blood

1776
Moves with family to Wales; the American colonies declare their independence from Britain; Thomas Jefferson writes the Declaration of Independence

1777
Returns with family to London

1778
Moves to Bath as companion to Mrs. Dawson

1780
Returns to London to nurse her mother

1782
Elizabeth Wollstonecraft dies

1784
Helps Eliza escape from marriage; establishes school at Newington Green

1785
Travels to Lisbon, Portugal to attend to Fanny Blood in childbirth; Fanny Blood dies; returns to London and breaks up her school

1786
Meets publisher Joseph Johnson; writes *Thoughts on the Education of Daughters*; takes up residence in Ireland as governess to Kingsborough family

1787

Writes *Mary, A Fiction;* writes but does not complete novel *The Cave of Fancy;* writes *Original Stories from Real Life;* moves to London to write for Joseph Johnson; U.S. Constitution drafted in Philadelphia

1789

French mob storms the Bastille prison in Paris; the French Revolution begins with the Declaration of The Rights of Man

1790

Writes *A Vindication of the Rights of Men* in response to Edmund Burke's *Reflections on the Revolution in France*

1791

Meets Thomas Paine, author of *Rights of Man,* and William Godwin at a dinner of publisher Joseph Johnson

1792

Writes *A Vindication of the Rights of Woman;* begins residence in Paris; Louis XVI executed; Jacobin "Terror" begins; war breaks out between France and England

1793

Writes *An Historical and Moral View of the Origin and Purpose of the French Revolution;* meets Gilbert Imlay

1794

Fanny Imlay is born; Robespierre and the Jacobin government falls; treason trials of English radicals in London begin

1795

Returns to London with daughter Fanny; attempts suicide; travels to Scandinavia; writes *Letters Written during a Short Residence in Sweden, Norway, and Denmark;* attempts suicide again

1796

Meets William Godwin again; begins writing but does not complete *The Wrongs of Woman; Or Maria*

1797

Marries Godwin; Gives birth to Mary Godwin; dies from complications of childbirth on September 10

FURTHER READING

MARY WOLLSTONECRAFT'S WORKS AND LETTERS

Todd, Janet, ed. *A Wollstonecraft Anthology*. Bloomington: Indiana University Press, 1977. Reprint, New York: Columbia University Press, 1989.

————. *Political Writings of Mary Wollstonecraft: A Vindication of the Rights of Men, A Vindication of the Rights of Woman, An Historical and Moral View of the French Revolution*. London: William Pickering, 1993.

————. *A Vindication of the Rights of Woman*. 1792. Reprint, edited by Miriam Brody, New York: Penguin, 1992.

Wardle, Ralph M., ed. *Collected Letters of Mary Wollstonecraft*. Ithaca, N.Y.: Cornell University Press, 1979.

Wollstonecraft, Mary. *A Short Residence in Sweden, Norway, and Denmark*. 1796. Reprint, edited by Richard Holmes, New York: Penguin, 1987.

————. *Maria, or the Wrongs of Woman*. 1799. Reprint, with an introduction by Anne K. Mellor, New York: Norton, 1994.

————. *Thoughts on the education of daughters; with reflections on female conduct, in the more important duties of life*. 1787. Reprint, edited by Gina Luria, New York: Garland, 1974.

————. *Mary, A Fiction*. 1788. Reprint, edited by Gary Kelly, London: Oxford University Press, 1976.

————. *Original Stories from Real Life, with conversations, calculated to regulate the affections, and form the mind to truth and goodness*. 1788. Reprint, New York: Woodstock, 1990.

————. *Posthumous Works of the Author of "A Vindication of the Rights of Woman."* Edited by William Godwin. 1798. Reprint, edited by Gina Luria, New York: Garland, 1974.

WORKS ABOUT MARY WOLLSTONECRAFT

Conger, Syndy McMillen. *Mary Wollstonecraft and the language of sensibility*. Rutherford, N.J.: Fairleigh Dickinson University Press, 1994.

Detre, Jean. *A Most Extraordinary Pair: Mary Wollstonecraft and William Godwin*. New York: Doubleday, 1975.

Falco, Maria J., ed. *Feminist Interpretations of Mary Wollstonecraft*. University Park: Pennsylvania State University Press, 1996.

Flexner, Eleanor. *Mary Wollstonecraft, a biography*. New York: Coward, McCann & Geoghegan, 1972.

George, Margaret. *One Woman's "Situation"*. Urbana: University of Illinois Press, 1970.

Godwin, William. *Memoirs of the Author of the Rights of Woman*. 1798. Reprint, edited by Richard Holmes, Harmondsworth, Middlesex, England: Penguin, 1987.

Jump, Harriet. *Mary Wollstonecraft: Writer*. New York: Harvester Wheatsheaf, 1994.

Jump, Harriet, ed. *Lives of the Great Romantics III: Godwin, Wollstonecraft and Mary Shelley By Their Contemporaries. Vol. 2, Wollstonecraft*. London: Pickering and Chatto, 1999.

Nixon, Edna. *Mary Wollstonecraft: Her life and times*. London: Dent, 1971.

Paul, C. Kegan. *William Godwin: His Friends and Contemporaries*. London: H.S. King, 1876.

Sunstein, Emily. *A Different Face: The Life of Mary Wollstonecraft*. New York: Harper and Row, 1975.

Tomalin, Claire. *The Life and Death of Mary Wollstonecraft*. New York: Penguin, 1992.

Wardle, Ralph M. *Mary Wollstonecraft, a critical biography*. Lawrence: University of Kansas Press, 1951.

Woolf, Virginia. "Mary Wollstonecraft." In *The Second Common Reader*. 1932. Reprint, New York: Harcourt Brace, 1986.

FICTIONALIZED ACCOUNTS RELATING TO WOLLSTONECRAFT'S LIFE AND PERIOD

Piercy, Marge. *City of Darkness, City of Light*. New York: Fawcett Columbine, 1966. (an account of the lives of notable women during the French Revolution)

Sherwood, Francis. *Vindication*. New York: Farrar, Straus & Giroux, 1993. (a novel based on Wollstonecraft's life)

WORKS ABOUT THE PERIOD IN WHICH WOLLSTONECRAFT LIVED

Brailsford, H. N. *Shelley, Godwin and their Circle*. London: Oxford University Press, 1951.

Hobsbawn, E. J. *The Age of Revolution 1789–1848*. London: Cardinal, 1989.

Kelly, Gary. *The English Jacobin Novel 1780–1805*. Oxford: Oxford University Press, 1976.

Marshall, Peter H. *William Godwin*. New Haven: Yale University Press, 1984.

Palmer, R. R. *Age of Democratic Revolution*. Princeton: Princeton University Press, 1959.

Thompson, E. P. *The Making of the English Working Class*. New York: Random House, 1963.

Thompson, J. M. *Robespierre and the French Revolution*. New York: Collier, 1966.

INDEX

Illustrations are indicated by page numbers in *italics*. The abbreviation MW is used for Mary Wollstonecraft.

ACKNOWLEDGMENTS

Many fine biographies and interesting reevaluations of Mary Wollstonecraft have attended her rescue as an important founding mother of the movement for women's rights. I am particularly indebted to the biography by Emily Sunstein for a sensitive interpretation of Wollstonecraft's life, rich in the detail that brings the late 18th century to life, and to Claire Tomalin for her helpful account of Wollstonecraft in Paris. Like so many others before me, I have depended as well on the annotated collection of Wollstonecraft's correspondence gathered by Ralph Wardle, who was also one of the first early biographers to bring her life to the attention of a new generation of scholars. All of these works were preceded, of course, by that first biographer of Mary Wollstonecraft, William Godwin, to whom all of us are indebted that he chose writing her life as a palliative for the grief he felt after her death.

As I revised this manuscript, I was grateful for the careful and timely reading of my young friend Sarah Eisenstein Stumbar, who suggested to me the questions her contemporaries might raise about Wollstonecraft's story. As always, when I write about the 18th century, I shared every comma and semicolon with Isaac Kramnick, who is almost as useful to me as the best reference collection, and considerably more fun. I relied early on and as the manuscript progressed on the interest, advice, and encouragement of both Nancy Toff, editorial director of the Children's and Young Adult Department of Oxford University Press, and Lisa Barnett, project editor, with whom I shared the privilege of using the Pforzheimer Collection at the New York Public Library.

PICTURE CREDITS

TEXT CREDITS

p. 20: From *The Collected Letters of Mary Wollstonecraft,* ed. Ralph M. Wardle (Ithaca, N.Y.: Cornell University Press, 1979), 59–60.

p. 37: From *The Collected Letters of Mary Wollstonecraft,* ed. Ralph M.Wardle. (Ithaca, N.Y.: Cornell University Press, l979), 66.

p. 61: From *Mary; Maria/Mary Wollstonecraft. Matilda/Mary Shelley,* ed. Janet Todd (New York: New York University Press, 1992) 7–8.

p. 82: From *A Vindication of the Rights of Woman* (1792; reprint New York: Penguin Classics, 1992), 133.

p. 102: From "An Historical and Moral View of the French Revolution," 1794; reprinted in *Mary Wollstonecraft/Political Writings,* ed. Janet Todd. (London: William Pickering, l993), 341.

p. 134: From *The Collected Letters of Mary Wollstonecraft,* ed. Ralph. M. Wardle. (Ithaca: Cornell University Press, l979), 395–396.

p. 139: From *Memoirs of the Author of the Rights of Woman,* ed. Richard Holmes. (London: Penguin, 1987), 276–277.

Miriam Brody is the editor of the Penguin edition of *A Vindication of the Rights of Woman* and the author of essays on Mary Wollstonecraft. She is also the author of *Manly Writing*, a study of gender and style in 18th-century schooltexts and in contemporary advice to writers. She is a professor in the Department of Writing at Ithaca College.